complete book of
yoga

complete book of
yoga

Vimla Lalvani

hamlyn

Contents

Introduction

The aspects of yoga tradition are vast and varied, and people correspondingly come to yoga for a variety of reasons. Some people suffer from stress-related conditions and have realized that yoga exercise is one way to release stress in the nervous system; some want only to tone their body and keep it youthful, while others aim to alleviate ailments such as migraine, backache, arthritis and rheumatism; some seek to develop their sexual relationships on a new plane; and some wish to use the principles of yoga philosophy to enrich their spiritual life. No matter what reason you are attracted to yoga you will reap all the benefits. You do not even need to believe in its philosophies - all you need to do is to practice it in order to gain the true benefits of this ancient science.

What is yoga?

Yoga is a holistic concept that unifies the physical, mental, spiritual, and emotional aspects of the self so that the person who practices it feels in total balance and in harmony with others as well as with his or her environment. It is an Ayurvedic science that teaches us how to live and function in life successfully.

The Vedic Scriptures are the oldest written verses ever recorded. Written thousands of years ago, they describe an ancient science that teaches us how to live life in harmony with the universe. From them are derived Ayurvedic medicine, a traditional Indian science of healing now increasingly popular in the West, and yoga *asanas* that help us purify our system and unite us to the cosmic Source.

Yoga is a Sanskrit word which means the union of mind, body, and soul. It follows from this that the individual person is a whole and must be viewed as such; the total integration of the mental, physical, emotional, and spiritual self is necessary in order to have a balanced life. There are five paths of yoga discipline, of which *Hatha* yoga is the first stage. The philosophy states that before you can discipline your mind in the art of meditation you must discipline your body first, Nirvana or spiritual enlightenment being your final goal. *Karma* yoga teaches us that good deeds bring us closer to God; *Bakti* yoga is devotional prayers and dedication of one's life to spiritual growth;

Gyana yoga is studying the philosophy of yoga and understanding the power of spiritual wisdom; and *Raj* yoga is the art of meditation that links us directly to a spiritual union with the Cosmic Energy. No matter which form of yoga that one chooses to practice the result will be the same; an understanding and belief in universal law and a deep understanding of the self. Even though your goal might not be a spiritual one you will find that you will feel more compassionate towards other people as well as being in tune with your environment.

This book is concerned with *Hatha* or physical yoga, which teaches us *asanas* or postures that discipline the mind and body. *Ha* means the sun, which represents masculine energy, and *Tha* means the moon, representing feminine energy. Each person, no matter which gender, has both masculine and feminine energies within himself or herself. *Hatha* yoga teaches us how to balance these energies in order to be in harmony with the universe. The *asanas* are held for as long as possible in order to build stamina as well as alter the energy in the body. We have seven chakras or energy centers in our torso and head that need to be unblocked so the energy flows evenly throughout the system. Twisting and turning the body forward, backward, and sideways stimulates all the nerves and internal organs and unblocks the chakras.

Breathing correctly as you perform the *asanas* constitutes a vital part of *Hatha* yoga. The *Pranayama* (breathing technique) increases the lung capacity, balances the masculine and feminine energies within the body and boosts energy levels. It calms and soothes the nervous system and acts as a natural tranquilizer so the person feels calm and relaxed.

A modern plague

There is a disease that is endemic in our society today: stress. Its effects range from making people tense and unhappy to causing irritable bowel syndrome, migraine, asthma, allergies, high blood pressure and heart attacks, as well as many other illnesses. It is even believed to contribute to cancer. Stress is not necessarily a bad thing: kept within bounds, it provides us with excitement, stimulation and motivation. However, in the modern world it often accelerates to dangerous levels. The major causes of stress are counted as bereavement, divorce, moving house and redundancy, and while bereavement was ever present in our lives family breakup and job losses, both forms of bereavement in themselves, are now commonplace. Add to that the sheer noise of life today, where a single home may have four televisions blaring in different rooms, burglar alarms on the house and car, a constantly ringing telephone and perhaps a flight path overhead and it's no wonder that stress levels become unbearable.

Yet even in these conditions, yoga can offer deep peace and relaxation. Just the deep breathing emanating from the diaphragm that yoga teaches has a tranquilizing effect, while the twisting and stretching of the *asanas* improves the circulation and sends fresh oxygen to the exhausted brain. Visualization and meditation techniques help to calm and focus the mind, providing a necessary distance from day-to-day worries. While a doctor may prescribe antidepressants or tranquilizers to help the individual cope with stress, this is but a short-term fix which may in itself have ill effects. Yoga, on the other hand, offers a life-long solution that brings with it a supple and toned body as a bonus.

Because of genetic differences, stress affects different people in different ways. It will manifest itself wherever there is a weakness in the system, so it is of utmost importance that each organ in the body receives an equal amount of blood and fresh oxygen in order to function properly. The deep breathing techniques in yoga send a fresh blood supply which revitalizes and rejuvenates all the internal organs, and combining this with twisting and turning the body into various positions assists the liver, kidney and spleen to eliminate harmful toxins which deplete energy and reduce the body's chance of functioning properly. If stress is not reduced or released from the internal organs, disease and decay set in, and as it is very difficult to reverse diseases it important to learn survival techniques to prevent illnesses from ever occurring to upset the natural balance of the body. However, where it is already too late to use yoga as a preventive measure for common ailments, remedial yoga offers practical quick fixes for instant relief.

Exploring the Tantra

There is nothing more rewarding in life than a truly loving relationship between two people, but when sexual problems or frustrations set in, even the best relationship in the world will suffer. Conversely, when the mind, body, and soul are truly integrated in each partner, sexual union is joyous and fulfilling. This ecstasy spills onto every level of the relationship and enhances not only a positive mental attitude for each person but boosts self-confidence and self-esteem. Both partners radiate love and happiness and there is an inner calm that permeates into all other relationships within the family, the workplace and social relationships.

Sexual energy is the most powerful energy in the body because it is this fundamental energy that creates life. When the base or first chakra is blocked, sexual tension can explode in a negative or violent way. It is important to release tension in the pelvic region and raise the energy to the highest or seventh chakra. When this is complete enlightenment is possible. Religious leaders often describe a spiritual union with God as divine bliss. The techniques of Tantric yoga teach you how to unblock all the energy centers so you reach a state of orgasmic ecstasy similar to a divine union with God.

Not only do the techniques of Tantra intensify the senses and sharpen sexual awareness, the practice of yoga also helps to resolve the emotional and psychological problems that are the usual underlying cause of sexual dysfunction. Yoga philosophy considers the sexual union of man and woman to be sacred, a part of universal love, and the spiritual ecstasy of yoga intensifies the physical thrill of sex.

The search for eternal youth

Since the beginning of time, the human race has been obsessed with searching for the fountain of youth. For centuries, elixirs and potions have been drunk and magical rituals have been practiced in order to ward off the ageing process. Today, millions of pounds are spent each year on cosmetics and cosmetic surgery with the hope that this will reverse the signs of ageing – but success is only limited.

However, even though we cannot stop the ageing process altogether we can certainly learn a way to outwit it so we can live longer and have better health. The secret of staying young is oxygenation. In yoga, breathing from the diaphragm increases the fresh oxygen that enters the bloodstream to purify and regenerate all the cells. This rejuvenates the entire system so the internal organs are functioning perfectly.

As you age, your metabolism and hormonal levels start to slow down and change. Practicing yoga exercises will help to maintain the same levels so your weight and your hormones remain stable. Added to this, the *asanas* improve circulation, tone the entire body, strengthen the back, energize and rejuvenate the entire system and maintain youthfulness so that you will feel fit and young. While yoga is used as a preventive measure to the signs of ageing it also relieves age-related conditions such as arthritis, rheumatism and osteoporosis. It helps to cure the insomnia and depression that often attend them as well as building the immune system to prevent further illness.

The mental attitude of people who are ageing is important – the saying that you are as old as you feel has a lot of truth in it. When someone is described as youthful you expect to see an invigorated person with boundless energy, sparkling eyes and a clear complexion. This is just what yoga can bring, with the exercises keeping your body supple, your skin toned and your mind alert.

Basic yoga principles

Stretching is the best way to achieve top-to-toe fitness as well as reducing stress in the muscle groups. In yoga exercise stretching is an integral part of each movement. The muscles are stretched lengthways, thus elongating them. This process eliminates the fat around each muscle so that it becomes toned, and this also helps to reduce the appearance of cellulite. People who practice yoga on a regular basis have long, lean muscles rather than bulk and always appear youthful and full of energy.

Perfect posture is an integral part of each movement and the yoga exercises are fluid and graceful. Imagine you are a dancer as you move smoothly from one exercise to the next. Never force or jerk your body – instead, allow the natural weight of the body to help you increase the stretch. Every single muscle in the body is working even as you stand tall. Visualize a string pulling you upwards from the top of your head and extend your arms from the shoulder blades as you stretch your arms out.

Yoga breathing begins from the diaphragm. As you inhale through the nose the stomach extends and as you exhale the stomach retracts. This method of breathing increases the lung capacity to its fullest so energy levels are increased instantly. A shallow breath does not circulate through the organs in the way that an intense breath is able to, and during yoga exercises the breath actually moves into the specific organ that is being stimulated. The end result of correct yoga breathing is thus a calmer mind and a relaxed and oygenated body.

Yoga is a discipline, so you must set a routine for yourself in order to achieve its benefits. Choose a time of the day when you can shut yourself off from the rest of the world. The postures might seem challenging at first, but with continued practice you will find yourself becoming more flexible so there will be a sense of joy as you tackle even the most difficult poses. As you become more advanced in your yoga practice you will feel a total feeling of inner calm. You will feel happy, healthy, and in total control of your destiny.

How to use the book

The book is divided into four sections, starting with a general one that introduces you to classic yoga *asanas* and moving on to three that focus on a particular aspect of life where yoga can bring you benefits.

Classic Yoga takes you through a beginners' course in which the exercises are very gentle, slow and easy to follow, as you learn to move and breathe in a new way. Once you are comfortable with these you can move onto the intermediate and advanced *asanas*, which will demand greater levels of stamina and suppleness to perform.

When you are suffering from stress your energy levels are depleted, so the **Yoga to Relieve Stress** section offers *asanas* for boosting your energy as well as for providing deep relaxation that will enable you to replace tension and anxiety with harmony and peace. Our most stressful moments often come outside the home, so there are simple five-minute *asanas* that can be done in the office and while travelling, as well as more complicated ones to do at home.

Yoga for Better Sex begins with a section that prepares the physical body for lovemaking and the mind for inner calm. The *asanas* here will tone your body, giving you increased stamina and flexibility so that you can embark upon the poses of the *Kama Sutra* without worrying about any physical strain. The *asanas* in the Prelude are designed to help you and your partner prepare together for physical union, equalizing your energy and attuning to one another by means of slow, flowing movements. These are followed by the Love Poses section, which shows you some of the classical movements from the *Kama Sutra* and describes them in detail so that you will find them easily achievable, leading you to fulfilling lovemaking.

The last part of the book, **Stay Youthful with Yoga**, presents a six-day workout that can be used lifelong to help you avoid many of the syndromes that come with advancing age. They are designed for specific areas and can be combined or just used according to your particular needs. Finally, there are remedial exercises you can do to alleviate some common age-related problems.

SAFETY NOTE

classic
yoga

This opening chapter includes specifically designed yoga sequences based on different levels of fitness and experience. The main objectives are to teach you the basics of yoga and to guide your progress through to an advanced level. The initial exercises provide a foundation course for total beginners, teaching the importance of breathing and alignment. These exercises are gentle, slow and easy to follow, and will teach you to move in a new way. The exercises progress to more dynamic poses which call for increased strength, stamina and suppleness. As you move into these more challenging yoga *asanas* you will feel a sense of elation in your ability to tackle difficult poses; you will become energized and motivated yet your mood will be calm. However, yoga is a discipline so only continued practice will show results. With dedication, the outcome can be dynamic: an invigorated body, increased stamina, improved muscle tone and a feeling of total harmony and calm.

Getting Started

No matter how unfit you are, you can safely begin the practice of yoga. Unlike modern exercise regimes, which are sometimes harsh and demanding, yoga will take you forward at a pace that your body can adjust to. However, as with all exercise, you should begin with a general warm-up so that your muscles are warmed and loosened, ready for stretching.

As you progress with yoga, you will find that your outlook on life becomes more positive. You will no longer experience serious mood swings or depression. As your concentration improves, you will be more organized and you will find yourself able to handle several tasks at the same time equally well.

Yoga philosophy offers people a scientific way of transcending their problems and suffering. It does not conflict with any religion or faith and can be practiced by anyone who is sincere and willing to discipline their life and search for truth. Little effort will bring immense returns like wisdom, strength and peace. As your awareness of your body increases, you will learn to listen to your 'higher self'. *Hatha* Yoga is the first step to spiritual enlightenment. However, the philosophy states that before you can discipline your mind and master the techniques of meditation, you must first discipline your body.

Many pupils of yoga find that they develop an interest in their own spiritual development; others do not. While some people concentrate only on balancing the mind and body, others find that they develop an insatiable need to go further. Each person is different and should follow their own inclinations. As you learn the positions and exercises in this book, you can decide for yourself how far you want to take your study of yoga.

Posture

Most people do not realize how important it is to stand and sit correctly. Bad posture is the main cause of chronic back pain and contributes to painful ailments such as slipped discs and sciatica. Invariably, people with bad posture lack energy and vitality. Their chests are slumped, and they do not breathe correctly as they use only a small portion of their lungs.

Yoga poses are designed to stretch the spine constantly and build the muscles in the lower back, enabling you to achieve perfect posture. You may think that you are standing or sitting correctly, but you may not understand your own body alignment. Indeed, pregnancy or either weight gain or loss can unbalance you.

Whether you are standing, kneeling or sitting, imagine that a string is pulling you upward from the top of your head. Push your shoulder blades down and lift the chest naturally. When you are in perfect posture, you will feel 'centered'. It is rather like placing building blocks on top of each other. If they are not evenly placed, they will tumble down.

The exercises in this book frequently refer to first and second position. In first position stand with your feet together and touching each other. Open the toes evenly and press your heels down. In second position stand with your feet approximately 30cm (1ft) apart. The feet should be positioned below the hips with the toes pointing forward.

1

Stand as tall as you can with your feet together, keeping your shoulders down and your stomach and tail-bone tucked in.

2

Raise your heels and balance on your toes. If you do not fall forward or backward you are in perfect posture.

In Steps 1 and 2, test yourself for perfect standing posture. (In Step 1, it is important to distribute your weight evenly.) Steps 3 and 4 demonstrate correct posture when kneeling and sitting.

3

4

Sit on your heels and place your hands on your knees. Now raise your spine, straightening your elbows.

Sitting cross-legged, lift the spine as far as you can. This centers your balance, creating a positive mental attitude.

Breathing

Breathing correctly is an integral part of yoga. All the movements you perform, if they are to be beneficial, require correct breathing. To breathe correctly means breathing through the nose from the diaphragm throughout all the exercises in this book, unless instructed otherwise. As we exhale from the diaphragm, our lung capacity increases and more oxygen reaches the bloodstream. This rejuvenates and revitalizes the cells, resulting in increased energy levels and a strong, healthy body.

When you are breathing correctly, you should breathe fluidly and evenly like a wave in the sea, flowing in natural rhythm. Take a few seconds to inhale and exhale. As you inhale the stomach extends outward and as you exhale the stomach contracts inward. As you practice you will notice that your breathing pattern increases in depth and duration and becomes very quiet.

In yoga you will use breathing techniques, known in Sanskrit as *pranayama*, that will balance the energies and focus the mind. Within the body there are seven energy centers known as chakras. *Pranayama* techniques unlock blockages so that

1

Place both hands on your stomach just below the waist and inhale slowly and evenly through your nose from the diaphragm. Feel your stomach distend as the diaphragm expands. Do not move your chest and shoulders.

the stream of energy flows smoothly from the base of the spine up to the top of the head to connect with the universal energy. When the subtle *prana*, or energy, is controlled, the body also comes under the mind's control and all imbalances are destroyed. If the body is strong and healthy, the energy flows freely.

Alternate Nostril Breathing (see page 149) shows you the difference between the masculine and feminine principle of energy. The right nostril is stronger, more fiery and more intense, i.e. masculine; the left is softer, cooler and more gentle, i.e. feminine. The alternate nostril technique combines the masculine and feminine energies to balance the entire system.

Deep breathing techniques act like a tranquilizer, calming the nervous system. The deeper you breathe, the stronger the effect and the more able you are to combat stress. *Pranayama* not only teaches willpower and self-control but also improves concentration and encourages spiritual development.

2

Exhale slowly and evenly and feel your stomach shrinking as your diaphragm contracts. As in Step 1, remember to resist moving your chest and shoulders.

Total Body Warm-up

A sedentary lifestyle and poor eating habits make many people feel lethargic. In addition, stimulants such as alcohol, caffeine and cigarettes clog up the system. The body needs help to eliminate these toxins. The Total Body Warm-up is devised to combat lethargy and cleanse the system.

This warm-up consists of ten gentle stages to awaken the body slowly, starting with movements which loosen and relax the muscles in the neck and shoulders. This sequence quickly restores energy and vitality, improving and strengthening every muscle in the central part of the body, especially the abdomen. The flexibility of the spine improves and circulation to the brain is increased. The waist, hips, abdomen, buttocks and thighs are all toned.

The stretches release tension in the muscle groups and prepare the body for the exercises that follow. As you perform the various steps, concentrate on exhaling, as this helps to relieve stiffness. Having completed the Total Body Warm-up you will feel calm, your eyes will glow and you will be filled with a sense of inner peace.

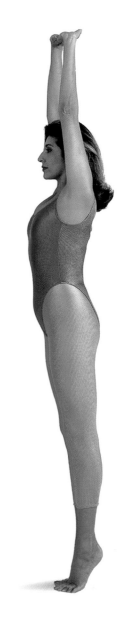

1

Stand tall with your feet together and your tail-bone tucked in. Inhale and raise your clasped hands above your head.

2

Breathing normally, balance on your toes with your eyes fixed ahead of you. Hold for 5 seconds, then return to Step 1.

4

Take your weight onto your heels, grasping the floor with your toes. Look up, thrusting your chest forward with all your strength. Inhale deeply.

3

Exhale and release your hands so that your arms are parallel. Hold for 5 seconds, then clasp your elbows behind your back.

5

Exhale. Push your hips forward and curve your spine backward. Open your chest and relax your throat and face muscles.

6

Inhale and exhale and stretch forward, leading with your chin. Keep your spine flat by lengthening from the tail-bone.

7

Holding your stomach muscles in, exhale and relax further and further forward, keeping your spine straight.

8

Breathing normally, release your arms from behind you, place your hands around your ankles and hold for 5 seconds.

9

Inhale deeply then slowly exhale as you stretch forward, resting your forehead on your knees. Try to place your torso as close as possible to your thighs. Hold for 5–10 seconds.

10

Part your feet to hip-width and straighten your spine from the tail-bone. Hold your elbows and stretch forward. Breathing deeply, hold for 10 seconds.

The Head Roll

The Head Roll relieves stiffness in the neck and shoulders. The exercise consists simply of rolling the head slowly in a circle without missing an inch. When the spine is not aligned properly you will experience tightness in the neck, shoulders or back. If this is the case, hold your position and breathe deeply to help the body return naturally to balance.

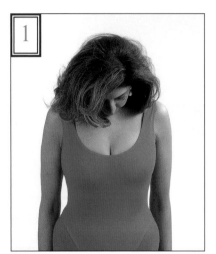

Keep your spine straight and drop your head forward, resting your chin on your chest. Breathe normally.

Roll your head gently up and round to the right. Try to keep your ear as close as you can to your shoulder.

Exhale and slowly roll your head to the left. Try to keep your shoulders down to allow freedom of movement.

Complete the circle by rolling your head down toward your chest. Repeat the exercise in the opposite direction.

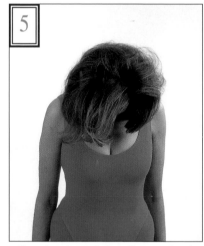

3

Continue the circle by rolling your head back. Relax the neck and throat and soften the face muscles, especially about the eyes.

Head and Shoulders

After releasing tension in the neck with the Head Roll, move on to this exercise which includes the shoulders and relieves stiffness throughout the entire length of the spine. The Head and Shoulders exercise can be done either standing or kneeling.

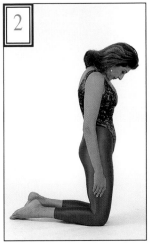

1

Kneel on the floor facing forward and inhale and exhale normally.

2

Drop your head forward, keeping your spine straight. Inhale.

4

Exhale. Tilt your head back and, looking up at the ceiling, rotate both shoulders backward together. Repeat the exercise 6 times.

3

Lift your elbows up behind you, resting your hands in the small of your back.

Salute to the Sun

This is a traditional Yoga warm-up, which has a wonderful, rejuvenating effect. The slow, gentle movements exercise and tone every muscle in the body and improve the body's flexibility, stamina, poise and suppleness. When performing Salute to the Sun, keep the energy flowing as you move from one position to another. Pay particular attention to your breathing pattern, as it is most important for increasing energy levels and vitality. Once you have managed to build up your stamina, you should aim to perform the

1

Breathe normally. Looking ahead, stand tall in perfect posture with palms together and shoulders down.

2

Inhale and step to the right. Fling your arms over your head and reach back behind you.

3

Exhale as you bring your feet together and relax down. Clasp the ankles and try to touch your knees with your forehead. Bend your knees slightly, if you wish.

4

Inhale and take the left leg back as far as you can with the toes tucked under, then flatten the leg as in Step 11. Raise your arms, with palms together. Breathe normally.

whole sequence ten times on each side.

As with all the previous exercises, Salute to the Sun should be performed with a graceful flow of energy. As you familiarize yourself with the sequence, you will eventually be able to move from one position to the next with confidence and fluidity, like a dancer.

Extend both legs behind you and raise yourself onto your hands and feet, keeping your arms straight.

Drop to your knees and keep your gaze straight ahead. Try not to make any unnecessary movements.

Sit back on your heels and stretch your arms forward to release your spine.

Inhale and dive forward like a serpent, with your chin sliding close to the floor. Bend your elbows.

9

Still inhaling, straighten your arms, swing forward with your hips and curve your spine, looking up.

10

Exhale, raise your hips, and drop your toes and heels down onto the floor, stretching the entire spine.

11

Inhale and bring your left leg forward, extending your right leg back (as for left leg in Step 4). Raise your arms, with palms together. Breathe normally.

12

Exhale and return to the position in Step 3 by leaning forward and bringing your right foot to join the left, clasping the ankles, then straightening the knees.

13

Inhale and step to the left. Stretch back,
looking up at the ceiling to release
tension in your back.

14

Exhale and return to Step 1. Repeat the sequence, this time
taking the opposite leg back in Steps 4 and 11.

The Jump

The Jump is a wonderful exercise that energizes and rejuvenates the entire body. Jumping increases the heartbeat and circulation, leaving you with a feeling of youth and vitality. Because this exercise is fairly strenuous, it is important to keep your breathing regular. Remember to always breathe through the nose.

1

Begin by standing tall in second position with arms raised above your head and fingers together, pointing up. Breathe normally.

2

Inhale, bend your knees, throw your arms forward and prepare to jump. Keep the knees parallel in line with your feet.

3

Exhale and jump as high as you can, throwing your arms back and with feet together. Repeat the exercise 6–12 times.

Beginners

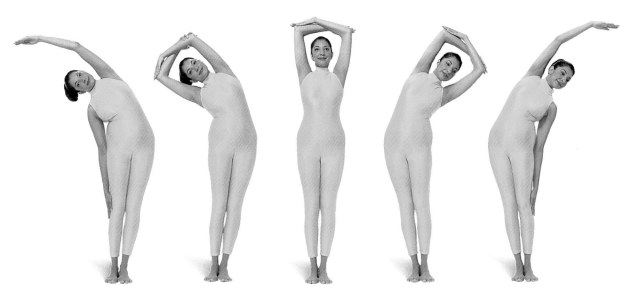

This section of the book is a foundation course for total beginners. It will teach you to balance your mental and physical energies and increase your flexibility and muscle tone, while improving your body shape and relaxing your nervous system.

Yoga is a science of movement: you should always begin with the Total Body Warm-up (page 22), and the exercises must be followed in their exact order. Here you are introduced slowly to the system with easy poses and stretches which will familiarize you with the yoga way of movement; you should pay special attention to details such as hand and feet positions.

Remember that even if you feel motionless, yoga is never static. Physical exercises like aerobics require a lot of energy, as every violent move burns it up; lactic acids are formed in the muscle fibers and this tires the muscles. The slow movements of yoga waste no energy; deep breathing allows more oxygen absorption and muscles suffer no fatigue.

Concentrate on what your body is doing. This is the first step toward disciplining the mind and body.

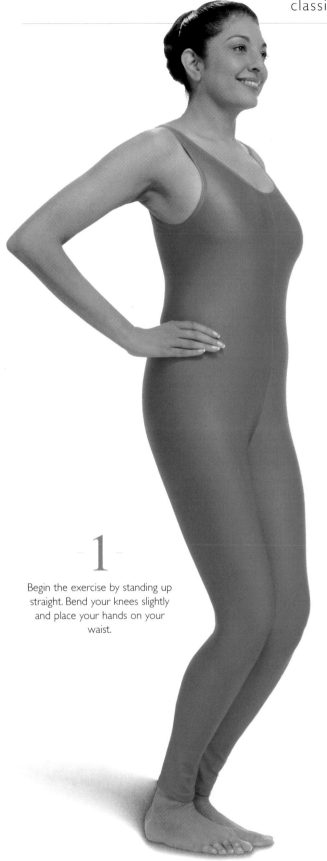

Head to Knee

This Head to Knee exercise lengthens the spine forward and is an excellent way to increase your body's flexibility and release unwanted body toxins. It helps soothe the nervous system, and will also relax the brain. You should never force your body forward, but as you increase the depth of your breathing you will be able to ease into the joy of deep stretching. It is very important to stretch forward from the waist. At the same time keep your back flat and don't round your shoulders. You might feel a pull in your hamstrings or some stiffness in the lower back. If this happens and you feel a bit dizzy, stretch your spine forward halfway, put your palms on a wall and keep your feet slightly apart.

1

Begin the exercise by standing up straight. Bend your knees slightly and place your hands on your waist.

2

Inhale and throw your arms forward, putting your head down between your arms. Bend your knees deeper and keep your head in line with your back.

3

Exhale and then throw your arms out straight behind your back, in line with your shoulders, but still keep your body in the same bent position.

4

Take your hands down and hold your ankles from behind, moving your head down toward your knees. Breathe normally for 5 seconds.

5

Now straighten your knees as much as you can. Pull your stomach muscles in, and drop your head down to your knees. Hold this position for at least 5–10 seconds. You'll feel the energy flow in a circular motion from your toes up the spine to your head. Uncurl and relax.

Dog Pose

This exercise is wonderful for stretching the whole body. Not only does it increase blood circulation, it also helps to tone and strengthen the legs and arms as well as curing fatigue and increasing your vitality. As with all the downward poses, it calms the nervous system and can be used as a relaxation pose if you're tired. Breathe deeply and evenly throughout the movements and relax your neck to release any tension in the shoulders.

Sit back on your heels with your toes curled under. Stretch out your arms in front of you and straighten your elbows. Place your forehead on the floor.

Inhale and kneel up, keeping your hands balanced out in front of you. Exhale and breathe normally. Stretch your fingers evenly on the floor, and keep your knees under your hips.

4

Now flatten your heels on the floor and move your thighs outward. Lift up your knees and stretch your spine upward. Straighten your arms and keep your shoulders down. Relax your face and neck, and breathe deeply for 30–60 seconds. As you gain flexibility, hold for longer. Relax and slowly stand upright.

3

Inhale, push the palms down and raise your hips upward. Stretch high onto your toes, pushing the shoulder blades down. Open out the chest and release the neck and shoulders. Bring your head in line with your spine and push your hips back. Hold for 10 seconds, while breathing normally.

The Tree

This pose focuses your mind and helps you learn how to concentrate and balance steadily on one leg. By balancing properly, you challenge your mind and you can unite your mental and physical energies. It also teaches you the importance of distributing your weight evenly between your heels and toes.

3

Now stretch your arms right up, while holding your balance for 5 seconds. Feel the energy move from your heels through your legs, into the spine and then through your arms and fingertips. Repeat on the other side.

1

Stand up straight. Place your right foot on your inner left thigh or close to the ankle or knee. Push out your hip but keep your hips square. Place your left hand on your left hip. Lift your standing leg as high as possible by stretching the muscle above the kneecap.

2

Look straight ahead and try to balance comfortably. When you are absolutely still, place your palms together and hold for 5 seconds. Grip the floor firmly with your toes so that the ankle does not move from side to side.

Side Stretch

Stretching to the side is an exercise that improves every muscle, joint, tendon and organ in the body. It also revitalizes the nerves, veins and body tissue by increasing the flow of oxygen to the blood. It helps cure sciatica, lumbago and other lower-back ailments. The body's strength and flexibility is heightened by the deep stretching, especially in the hip joints, waist and torso.

1

Stand up straight and place your feet about 1m (3ft) apart. Stretch out your arms with your palms facing down. Keep them in line with your shoulders. Breathe normally.

2

Turn in your left foot slightly and point your right foot 90° to the right. Inhale and stretch to the right. Keep the spine straight and do not tilt forward. Breathe normally and hold for 5 seconds.

3

Place your right hand on your right ankle and extend your left arm up in a straight line with your palm facing forward. Look up toward your arm, keeping your head up. Relax your face and shoulders, and hold for 10 seconds.

4

Take the left arm over and bend to the right to feel the additional stretch. Turn your head forward and keep your weight on your back heels to maintain an equal stretch on both sides of the torso. Hold for 5 seconds.

5

Return to Step 1. Bring your arms to your sides, placing your right arm on your right leg. Kneel on your left knee. Stretch the right leg out, pointing the toes. Balance evenly.

6

Inhale deeply and stretch out the right leg as far as possible without tilting forward. Stretch your left arm over to the right and feel the pull in your side. Keep your head balanced between your arms. Exhale and breathe normally.

7

Now sit on the floor, stretch out your right leg and fold your left leg in front, placing your foot on your inner right thigh. Clasp your right hand around your right foot and flex your thumb. Bend your right elbow and stretch forward toward the knee.

8

Inhale, take your left arm over your head and try to reach your right thumb with your fingers. Keep turning your upper torso to the side and keep your head evenly balanced. Increase the stretch and hold for 5 seconds.

9

Exhale and relax your head and arms down over your right knee. Keep your right foot flexed and, as you breathe normally again, relax your body further down toward the floor.

10

Lift your head up and stretch your legs out as wide as possible. Inhale and as you exhale stretch forward with your arms to reach your heels, or just reach for your thighs, knees or ankles. Stretch with your spine straight. Breathe deeply and hold for 10 seconds.

11

Now relax your head down toward the floor. Stretch your arms out, while keeping the toes flexed. Breathe normally and turn your knees upward, but push down. Hold for 15 seconds. Repeat on the other side.

The Warrior

The Warrior pose is dynamic in its approach, and its aim is to develop a positive mental attitude and to give you physical control over your body. The Warrior is the basis for all standing postures, so the exact positioning of your spine, arms, legs and feet is very important. Hold your spine very straight as you open out your chest.

1

Stand up straight, feet together, and bend your knees slightly in preparation to jump. Bring your arms up to shoulder level and place your fingertips together.

2

Jump to open your legs wide – they should be about 1.2m (4ft) apart. Make sure your toes are pointing forward and stretch both your arms out sideways.

3

Turn your right knee and foot to the right. Lean your body backward and push your hips and stomach forward. Now bend your right knee, keeping your spine straight. Bend further until there is a 90° angle between your thigh and the floor. Repeat on the other side.

The Eagle

The Eagle exercise focuses your mind so that you can concentrate on attention to detail. It grounds your energy and improves your balance. It can help to eliminate any cellulite and extra fat around the thighs, and also tones the leg, arm, and calf muscles. As you do the exercise, always keep your eyes fixed ahead on one spot to help you maintain your balance.

1

Stand up straight. Hold your left hand, facing upward, in front of your nose and stretch out your right arm. Focus on one spot straight ahead. Breathe normally.

2

Bend both your knees and wrap the right leg around the left. Try to wrap the right foot around the left ankle. The deeper you bend the easier it is to wind your leg.

3

Bring your right arm under your left, crossing them at the elbows, but keeping your shoulders down. Twist your right hand toward your left palm in front of your nose and press palms together. Keep your shoulders even, but press down to open the chest. Breathe normally, holding as long as possible. Repeat on the other side.

Sitting Twist

If you practice these twisting movements regularly, any pain that you are suffering in your lower back will rapidly diminish. The muscles of your neck will also be strengthened, especially when you look over the shoulder (not shown) and any tension is released from your spinal system. Your liver and spleen are activated by the movements and the size of your abdomen is reduced in the twisting position.

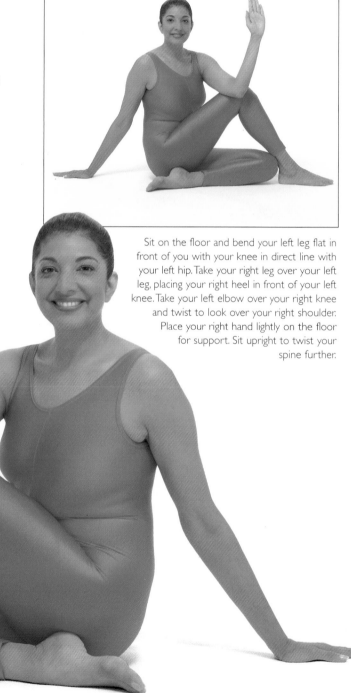

1

Sit on the floor and bend your left leg flat in front of you with your knee in direct line with your left hip. Take your right leg over your left leg, placing your right heel in front of your left knee. Take your left elbow over your right knee and twist to look over your right shoulder. Place your right hand lightly on the floor for support. Sit upright to twist your spine further.

2

Repeat the exercise on the other side. Make sure the palm of your raised arm is facing up with the fingertips together.

Toe Pull

This Toe Pull exercise stretches the body forward from the hips, helps to strengthen the leg muscles and increases the flexibility of the hamstrings and the spine. The movement stimulates the kidneys, liver and pancreas as you pull in the abdominal muscles. It also helps to flatten the stomach.

Sit upright with your legs out in front of you. Flex both feet and raise your arms over your head. Hold onto your elbows, keeping your shoulders down. Breathe normally.

Bend forward from the hips, keeping the back flat. Try not to curve your spine. Hold up your chin, keeping your head balanced between your arms. Hold for 5 seconds.

Reach further forward and try to grasp two fingers around your big toes. Flex the thumbs and keep the elbows straight. Inhale and exhale, and hold for 5 seconds.

Bend your elbows and stretch forward, pointing your chin. Keep your back flat and your head out in front. Breathe deeply and hold for 10 seconds.

Flat Twist

The Flat Twist relieves any tension that gets trapped in the neck and shoulders. It also alleviates lower back pain and is a really good stretching exercise for your spine. Remember to keep both shoulders flat on the ground and always look in the opposite direction to your feet to increase the body stretch.

1

Lie flat on the ground and take your arms out to the side, placing your palms facing down. Put your left heel on top of the toes of the right foot. Breathe normally.

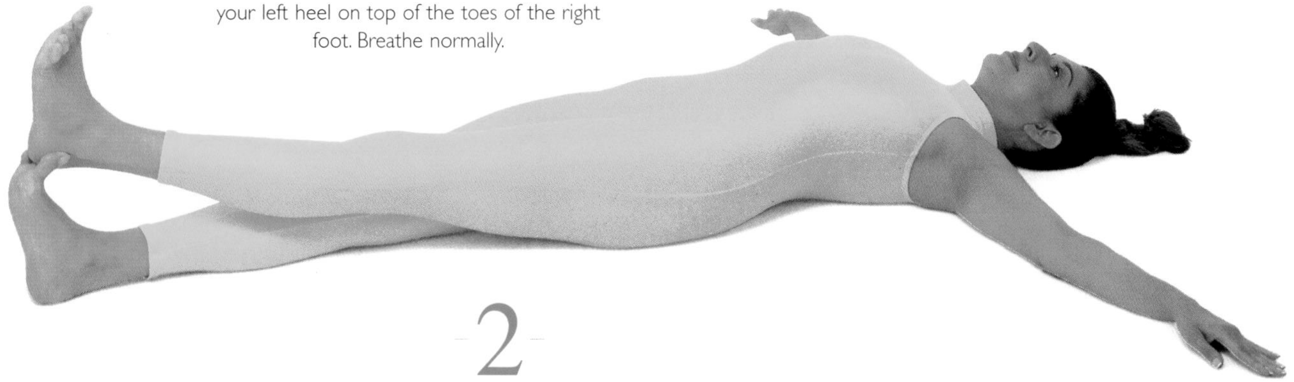

2

Inhale and as you exhale twist both feet to the right and look over your left shoulder. Hold the position for 5 seconds.

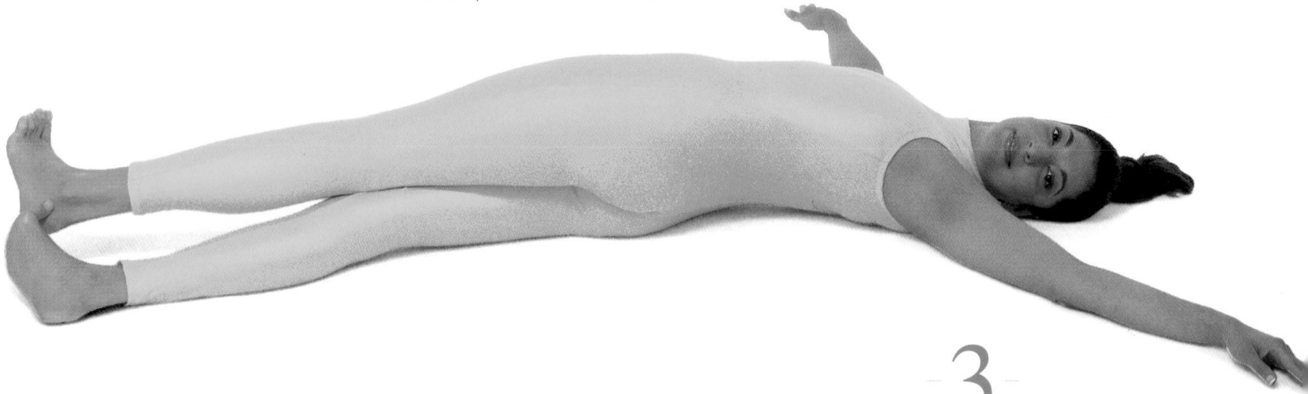

3

Bend your knees into your chest to increase the stretch, keeping legs and feet together. Inhale as your legs come up and then exhale and twist to the left. Relax onto your back and repeat on the other side.

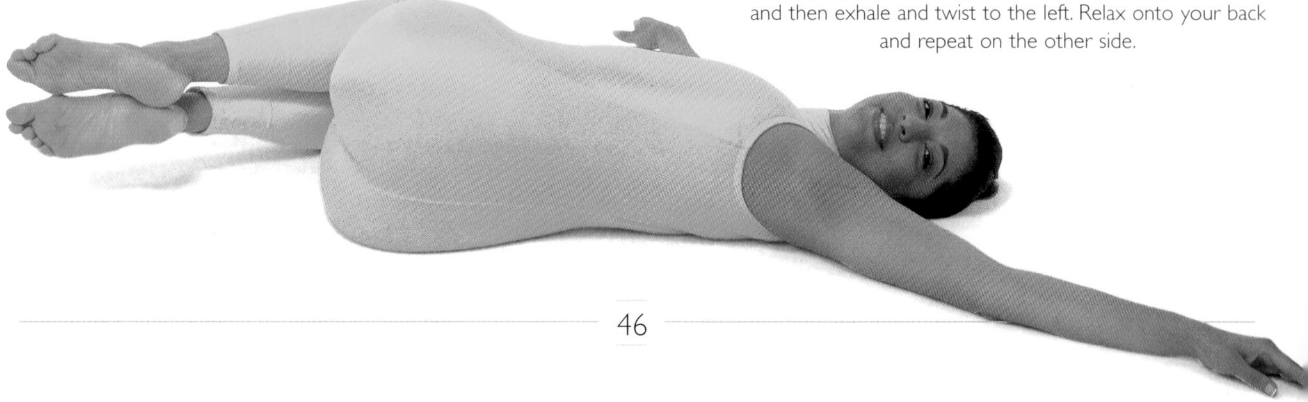

The Fish

When you do the Fish exercise you'll tone the stomach and leg muscles as well as releasing tension in the neck and shoulders. It also improves circulation to the face and slows the ageing process. These movements strengthen the lower back and open out the chest, increasing your lung capacity, which improves conditions such as bronchitis and asthma.

Lie on the floor with your arms out and point your toes. Inhale and raise your chest, resting your weight on the crown of your head. Feel the stretch in your neck and face. Exhale and breathe normally, holding for 3 seconds.

Still balancing on your head, inhale and raise your right leg, keeping your hip on the floor. Place your palms together above your chest, holding for 3 seconds. As you exhale, lower your leg slowly. Relax to the floor, if necessary, before Step 3.

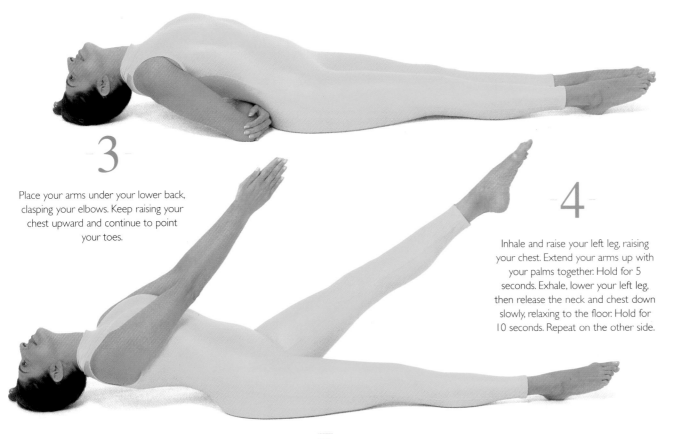

3

Place your arms under your lower back, clasping your elbows. Keep raising your chest upward and continue to point your toes.

4

Inhale and raise your left leg, raising your chest. Extend your arms up with your palms together. Hold for 5 seconds. Exhale, lower your left leg, then release the neck and chest down slowly, relaxing to the floor. Hold for 10 seconds. Repeat on the other side.

Back Bend

All back bends strengthen the spine and open
out the chest cavity to improve deep breathing.
The movement increases blood circulation and
raises energy levels. Even though back bends
are strenuous to do, it is very important to keep
your face relaxed and free of tension throughout.
You will feel exhilarated in Step 4 as your
whole body, especially your arms and legs, is
strengthened. The deep breathing technique will
also give you a feeling of complete calm.

2

Inhale and sit up tall, stretching your
arms upward in line with the side of
your head. Stretch out your legs slightly,
but keep your feet together.
Breathe normally.

1

Lie flat on the floor and bring your knees
up. Place your feet as close to your body
as possible. Stretch both your arms out
behind your head and breathe normally.

3

Keeping your feet flat on the floor, balance your arms behind you. Place your palms in opposite directions to your feet to support your body weight. Inhale and lift your buttocks, keeping an even line between your knees, hips and shoulders. Look up, exhale and breathe normally for 5 seconds.

4

Inhale, extend your legs and straighten your knees. Drop your head back and relax the neck and face. Keep pushing your hips upward. Breathing normally, hold for 5 seconds.

The Cobra

The Cobra strengthens and tones the lower back muscles. It alleviates back pain and prevents other common back ailments. The action of the Cobra tightens the buttock muscles and increases the intra-abdominal pressure which tones the uterus and ovaries. It also regulates the menstrual cycle and helps the thyroid and adrenal glands to work more effectively.

Lie flat on your stomach with your feet together. Point your toes, bend your arms close to your body, and place your palms flat under your shoulder blades. Point your chin downward.

2

Inhale and raise your head off the floor. Place your hands on the floor with your elbows inward. Keep your chin up and make sure your hip bones stay on the floor. Breathe normally and hold for 10 seconds. On the last exhalation, slowly lower yourself to the floor and return to Step 1. Repeat.

Return to Step 1, but this time place your hands under the breastbone and point your elbows outward.

4

Inhale, push down and lift your body off the floor. Look upward, keeping your shoulders down and your hips just off the floor. Breathing normally, hold for 10 seconds. On the last exhalation, slowly lower yourself and relax.

Back Lift

This exercise is rather strenuous to do and your body needs to be correctly aligned to achieve the right results. Not only does this type of lift tone the legs, buttocks, and stomach muscles, it also strengthens the lower back to enable you to sit and stand with perfect posture. Both your hip bones and shoulder blades should remain on the floor to stop you moving from side to side throughout the exercise. As a beginner you need not worry about the height of your leg lift, but as you gain strength and continue practicing, your hips will become more flexible and you will be able to lift your legs even higher.

Lie on the floor face down. Keep your back straight and place your arms by your sides, holding your hands as fists. Inhale and raise your left leg, keeping your hips square. Breathe normally and hold for 6 seconds. On the last exhalation slowly lower the leg, then inhale and repeat on the other side.

2

With your feet together, raise your hips slightly off the floor with your elbows resting under the hip bones. Keep your hands in fists, balanced under the thighs for support.

Inhale and raise your legs. Place your forehead on the floor. Keep lifting, breathing deeply, for as long as you can. On the last exhalation lower both legs. Repeat, then turn your head to one side and relax.

Soles of Feet

This Soles of Feet movement opens up the hips and increases flexibility in the hip joints, knees and thighs. Rotating the legs outward helps to increase the body's suppleness and also improves overall posture and mobility of the spine. It is an ideal exercise to do in preparation for giving birth, but take care not to bounce or jerk the spine.

1

Sit up tall on the floor with your legs in front of you. Bring the soles of your feet together and reach forward to place your hands around your ankles.

2

Bring the heels closer into your body and sit upright. Relax your shoulders, then stretch up from the pelvis and open out the chest.

3

To increase the stretch of the hips, thighs and knees, place your elbows over the knees. Bend over, curving your spine and keeping your shoulders down. Inhale, and as you exhale push your knees to the floor. Breathe and relax into the stretch, slowly lowering your head to your feet.

Intermediate and Advanced

By now you have become familiar with the general style of yoga exercises and you have gained more flexibility, strength and stamina. You are now ready to twist your body in various ways, remembering, of course, to start with the Total Body Warm-Up (see page 22).

Intermediate and advanced poses are more physically and mentally challenging. The exercises are dynamic and you will experience the energy flowing from one position to another. The muscles, joints and blood vessels will all be stretched, so that the blood is equally distributed to every part of the body and more energy flows into the relaxed muscles.

Try to hold the postures for longer with a calm and still mind. This gives time for the mind to focus and the body to cleanse, purify and build the system.

Vinyasa

Vinyasas are a series of different movements done in an active and dynamic style. Their function is to increase the stamina and strength of the body and to have an aerobic effect on the heart. Consequently, they are meant to be strenuous in nature and I have specifically designed this series to challenge your skill and to encourage you to develop grace through dynamic movement. Pay attention to the exact postures and do not rush. Breathe deeply and evenly through each of the positions.

1

Stand tall with your feet in second position directly under your hips and your knees bent. Inhale and throw your arms forward in parallel position.

2

Exhale, place your hands on the floor and jump, taking your feet out behind you. Stretch your spine and keep your legs and arms straight. Breathe normally.

3

Inhale, lift your heels and rise onto your toes. Change your foot position and balance on the front of your toes. Lower your hips toward the floor and raise your spine. Keep your shoulders down and look up. Breathe normally.

5

Exhale and place your left arm back down to the floor and swing your hips toward the floor. Tuck your toes under and point both hands forward, under the shoulder blades. Breathe normally.

4

Keeping your body in a straight line, turn your right hand to the front and your legs and feet together to the side. Raise your hips to maintain the straight line and raise your left arm, palm facing forward. Breathe deeply and hold for a few seconds.

6

Drop to your knees and begin to relax your spine. Breathe deeply.

7

Take your hips all the way back to your heels. Stretch your arms out in front of you. Breathe deeply and relax for a few moments.

8

Keeping your hands in the same position, inhale and dive down, leading with your chin and moving your chest smoothly as close to the floor as possible.

9

Exhale, sweep the spine forward and come up into the Cobra pose. Breathe normally.

10

Inhale and return to the one-arm balance as in Step 4, but on the other side. Make sure your alignment is correct. Breathe normally and try to hold still for as long as you can.

11

Exhale and return to Step 5. Inhale and return to Step 2. Breathing normally, increase the stretch.

12

Inhale and raise your right leg in a straight line behind you. Point the toes, hold, and breathe deeply. Repeat on the other leg.

13

Walk your hands back to your feet. Bend your knees and balance on your toes. Straighten your spine and hold for a few seconds. Return to standing position and repeat the entire series.

Half Lotus

This exercise is a wonderful challenge because it combines balance with concentration. In all difficult standing postures it is essential to keep the weight-bearing leg absolutely still when progressing through the various movements. Make sure the leg is pulled up as high as possible by gripping the floor with your toes and lifting the muscle above the kneecap.

1

Stand up straight. Lift your right foot up and bring your heel as close as possible to the left hipbone. Breathe normally.

2

Push your right foot against your left leg and balance your weight on your left leg.

3

Bring the palms together to help focus your attention. Make sure your shoulders are down and your face is relaxed.

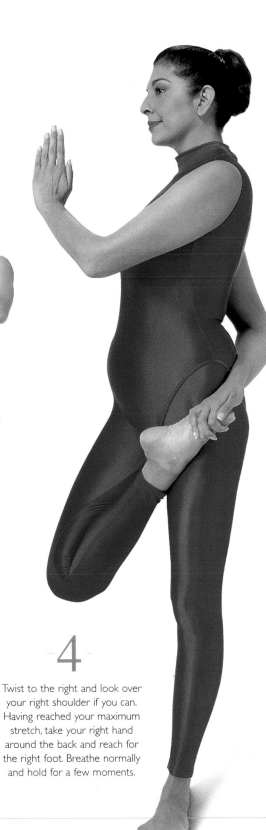

5

Release the foot and return to center position. Change legs and repeat on the other side.

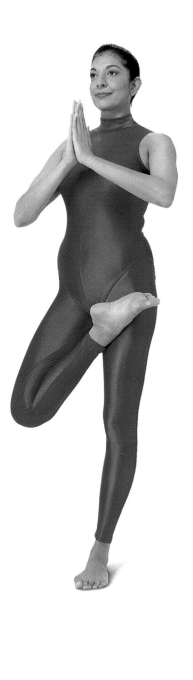

4

Twist to the right and look over your right shoulder if you can. Having reached your maximum stretch, take your right hand around the back and reach for the right foot. Breathe normally and hold for a few moments.

Leg Extension

This position gives you more
flexibility of the spine and builds
strength in your lower back and
legs. It opens the hips and makes you
slimmer around the hips. It is also a
difficult balancing exercise that focuses
your concentration. The final position is quite
hard to master, but don't be discouraged if you
can't get your forehead right down to your knee.

1

Stand up straight with your
feet together. Bend forward
and grasp your ankles.
Breathe normally.

2

Place both hands on the floor in front of you and focus
on one spot on the floor. Inhale and pull your stomach
muscles up, while raising your left leg as high as
possible. Keep the knee straight and point your toes.
Breathe normally.

3

Still concentrating hard, take your hands to your right ankle and keep lifting the kneecap up. Open your toes and grip the floor. Breathe normally.

4

Keep stretching your leg out behind you as you pull your head toward your knee. Try to hold for as long as possible, pointing your toes upward, then slowly return to an upright position. Repeat on the other side.

The Tower

This series of movements increases the strength in your legs and also makes your spine more flexible. It expands the chest, helping you to breathe more deeply and improving your lung capacity. The exercise also helps to relieve any stiffness in the neck and shoulders and make them more supple. At the end of the Tower, when your head is resting on your knee, the abdominal organs are toned and cleansed. This is because your deep breathing has pumped fresh oxygen into the blood, increasing the circulation and revitalizing and purifying them.

Stand upright with your feet about 1m (3ft) apart and your toes pointing forward. Take your arms up so that your palms face each other and straighten your elbows, keeping your shoulders down. Breathe normally.

Turn your left foot to a 90° angle, while moving the right foot slightly inward. The heel of the left foot should be in line with your right instep. Keep your head evenly balanced between your arms.

Bend your left leg so that your thigh is parallel to the floor. Throw your arms up and cross your thumbs with your palms together. Look upward and arch your spine. Breathe deeply and hold for 8 seconds.

4

Straighten your head between your arms and move your body forward with your weight on your left leg. Keep your leg, spine and arms in a straight line. Breathe deeply and hold for 8 seconds.

5

Relax down to the floor and place your hands on the floor. Drop your head to your knee. Keep breathing normally.

6

With your head still at your knee and with your palms on the floor, inhale and straighten the knee as much as possible. Breathe normally and hold for 8 seconds. Return to Step 1 and repeat on the other side.

Deep Lunge

The Deep Lunge exercises every muscle and tendon in the body. The intensity of the side stretch trims the thighs, hips and waistline, invigorates the internal organs and soothes the nerves. The position of the spine in relation to the hips helps to balance the endocrine system – the pituitary gland, thyroid, gonads and pancreas, all of which are glands that secrete hormones – as well as releasing toxins that build up in the system.

-1-

Adopt the Warrior pose (page 42), making sure your left leg makes a 90° angle and the back of your knee is in line with your heel. You can take the right leg further out to increase the lunge. Breathe normally.

-2-

Take your left hand down to your left ankle, turn your upper body and look over your right shoulder, twisting as much as possible. Place your right hand on the inner left thigh to increase the twist. Breathing deeply, hold for 8 seconds.

3

Place your left palm down on the floor and extend your right arm, elbow straight, close to your ear. Keep looking upward. Breathing deeply, hold for 8 seconds.

4

Inhale and raise your body, keeping your spine in the same position. Clasp your hands together over your head and stretch upward. Breathing deeply, hold for 8 seconds, then return to Step 1. Straighten the knee and repeat on the other side.

Side Lunge

This series of movements increases flexibility of the spine, improves balance and tones and cleanses the abdominal organs. You may feel dizzy or nauseous during the exercise, but this is a good sign – it means you are releasing toxins in the system. Just stop if you feel in any way uncomfortable and breathe deeply to regain your equilibrium. Always stretch from the tail bone and keep your hips and torso square to the side.

Exhale and, keeping your spine straight and your chin up, lower yourself to a 90° angle to the floor.

Still exhaling, bend and rest your forehead on your knee. Keep both legs straight – lift the muscles above the kneecaps to maintain balance. Breathing normally, hold for 6 seconds.

1

Follow feet positions in Steps 1 and 2 of Side Stretch (page 39). Place your palms together behind your lower back or toward the mid-back. Push the elbows toward each other and open the chest. Look up and bend back as far as possible. Inhale deeply.

Bend your left knee and lunge forward. Drop your head down on the inner side of the knee. Breathe deeply and hold for 6 seconds.

Straighten your knee, relax your arms down and place your hands on the floor, palms down. Breathe deeply and hold for as long as you can.

Inhale and raise your body so that your back is flat, with your arms back and upward. Breathing normally, hold for 6 seconds.

7

Return to an upright position, take your feet and arms through the center as in Step 1 of Side Stretch and repeat on the other side.

Front Lunge

This exercise is beneficial both mentally and physically. Stretching forward from the hips calms and soothes the central nervous system, lifts fatigue, refreshes the mind and invigorates the blood circulation. The flexibility of the hamstrings, hips and spine is improved and the leg muscles are toned. Make sure that you always stretch forward from the tail bone and hold your stomach muscles up. Keep your spine straight throughout the exercise and breathe deeply from the diaphragm in order to increase the relaxing effect.

1

Stand tall with your feet 1.2m (4ft) apart. Place your hands on your hips. Inhale and as you exhale move your torso forward to flat-back position, keeping your chin up.

– Tips –

+ Pay attention to your breathing, and take care not to hold your breath.

+ Push your weight onto your heels and grip the floor with your toes in order to steady your balance.

+ Keep your fingertips together in Step 4.

+ Whenever you straighten your legs, lift the leg muscles above the kneecap in order to avoid injury.

Still exhaling, relax forward, placing your hands on the floor. Push your weight to your heels, raise your hips back, grip the floor with your toes; open your fingers and stretch your spine.

Walk your hands back and distribute your weight evenly between your heels and toes. Lift your chin and keep your back straight.

4

Inhale and raise your arms evenly on both sides. Keep your elbows straight and your fingertips together. Breathe deeply and hold for 6 seconds.

▶

5

Relax your arms and drop your forehead down toward the floor. Breathe normally.

6

Inhale and clasp your hands around your ankles. Exhale and stretch your forehead down toward the floor. Breathe normally and hold for 6 seconds. Make sure your arms and legs are straight.

8

7

Bend your elbows and relax your knees. Push your palms down on the floor and prepare to jump into first position.

Inhale and jump. Breathe normally and balance on your toes. Steady yourself by placing your fingertips on the floor. Straighten the legs first, then the spine, and stand in perfect posture.

Standing Bow

This graceful exercise, called the Standing Bow because of the curve of the spine, will give you a sense of elation and power when you hold the pose as long as possible. The energy is continuously flowing in a circular pattern and as you increase the stretch your breathing pattern will quicken. Breathe deeply from the diaphragm to increase energy levels. This exercise will rejuvenate your spine and give you a sense of joy. Your circulation will be greatly improved and your whole body toned.

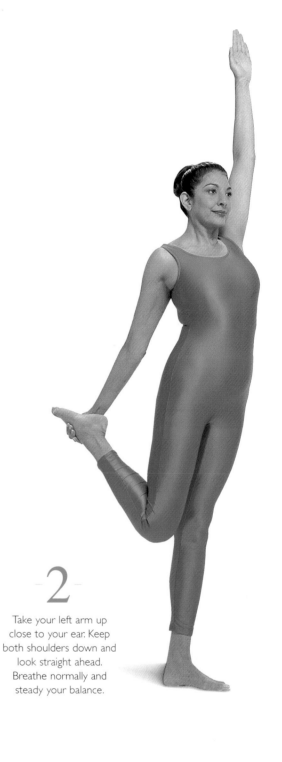

1

Stand up straight with your arms at your sides. Take your right leg behind you and hold the inner side of your foot. Straighten your elbow.

2

Take your left arm up close to your ear. Keep both shoulders down and look straight ahead. Breathe normally and steady your balance.

4

Move your upper body forward smoothly and keep stretching your back leg upward. Breathe deeply. Imagine you are an elastic band and continue to stretch until the toe of your raised leg is directly above the top of your head, or until your energy snaps and releases. Repeat on the other side.

3

Inhale, lift the right leg up from the hip as high as possible and then extend the left arm forward. Breathing normally, stretch in opposite directions.

The Letter T

Performing Letter T is very challenging and builds
up your strength and stamina. It is a powerful and
dynamic stretch and is the only asana that should
not be held longer than 10 seconds. It increases
your pulse rate and you will feel
your breath coming more
quickly. The stretching
also firms your buttocks
and upper arms.

3

As you exhale stretch out from your tail
bone in both directions. Keep stretching
your spine forward and keep pointing
your toes behind you until you reach a
perfect Letter T. Deepen your breathing
and hold the position for up to
10 seconds. Repeat on the other side.

1	2
Stand up straight with your feet together. Raise your arms above your head. Place your palms together and straighten your elbows. Push your elbows back behind your ears, keeping your shoulder blades down. Breathe normally.	Inhale deeply and point your right leg out behind you. Keep both your right knee and your spine straight as you stretch out. Focus on one spot in front of you to help you to keep your balance.

-Tips-

+ It is important to breathe deeply from the diaphragm during the final position to increase your energy levels and vitality.

+ Point your toes as much as possible. This will help you to keep your knee and foot in a straight line.

+ Keep pointing your toes and stretching your arms forward at the same time. Imagine you are a rubber band being stretched in opposite directions.

Shoulder Stand

This is one of the most important asanas in classical yoga. Its benefits are many, the most important being that it stimulates and regulates the thyroid and parathyroid glands. Because of the chinlock, menstrual cycles regularize and weight remains stable. Healthy blood flows through the neck and chest, curing respiratory ailments and preventing sinus troubles and colds. Daily practice of this exercise cleanses the bowels and eliminates toxins.

2
Exhale and raise your legs to a 90° angle with your body, pointing your toes.

3
Inhale and take your legs over your head until your toes touch the ground. Inhale and exhale.

1
Lie flat on the floor with your arms at your sides. Inhale and bring your knees into your chest.

5

Bend your knees and bring the soles of your feet together.

4

Inhale and raise both legs as high as possible – the aim is to straighten the spine completely. Lock your chin, point your toes and place your hands in the small of your back to support your spine. Hold for 30 seconds, breathing normally.

▶

6

Straighten both legs behind you.
Tuck your toes under and, breathing deeply,
walk both feet to the right
side of your head.

7

Drop both knees as close to your right ear
as possible. Straighten both legs and walk
your feet to the left, then drop your knees as
close to your left ear as possible.

8

Bring both legs directly behind your head. Point your
toes. Inhale and raise both legs directly parallel to the
floor. Breathe normally.

9

Bend both knees and change the position of your hands, so your thumbs are on your tail bone and your fingers are on your waist.

10

Straighten your spine and split your legs, creating a 90° angle with your left leg. Repeat on the other side.

11

Return to the classic
Shoulder Stand and
hold for 10 seconds.

12

Bend your right leg and place
the outer side of your foot
against your left thigh just
above your knee.

14

Return to the classic
Shoulder Stand and hold
for 10 seconds.

13

Bring your right heel toward
your left hipbone. Push the knee
back so that it is square with
the left hip. Return to Step 11
and repeat 12 and 13 on the
other side.

17

Twist the entire spine to the left. Return to center and rotate to the right side.

16

Push both hips back so they are square.

15

Begin the lotus position. Bend your right leg and with your left hand pull the right foot in as close to the left hipbone as possible. Repeat on the other side.

18

Return to the classic
Shoulder Stand. Hold for
5–10 seconds.

19

Repeat Step 10 but extend the right leg.
Point the toes of both feet.

20

Drop your left foot to the floor and point your right leg upward.

21

Bend your right knee and place both feet on the floor. Raise your hips as high as possible. Breathe normally.

22

Take your hands down to
the floor and continue to
raise your hips.

23

Exhale slowly and, working from the top of
the spine, slowly lower one vertebra at a
time until your spine is completely flat
on the floor.

24

Relax your legs down to the floor and
release your spine into the deep relaxation
or Dead Man's pose. Relax for 5 minutes.

The Wheel

The Wheel, Bow (page 92) and Camel (page 93) are intense back bends that invigorate the spine, alleviate back pain and increase lung capacity. We rarely stretch backward and these positions release fear and bestow a positive outlook on life. All three asanas release energy in the body's cells, glands and organs. The Wheel also builds muscle tone in the legs, hips, shoulders, arms, wrists and hands. Holding the position will build strength and give stamina to the spine and limbs.

Lie flat, knees bent and in line with your hips, and feet flat and as close to the buttocks as possible. Inhale and raise your buttocks as high as possible. Try to hold on to your ankles. Breathe normally. Lower down and repeat.

Keeping your feet in the same position, lift your hips and buttocks and take your arms over your head with palms facing downward. Push up and rest on the crown of your head. Breathe normally and hold for 5–10 seconds.

3

Lift as high as possible, balancing on your toes and hands. Straighten your elbows and, breathing normally, hold for as long as possible. Return to Step 2, lift your head toward your chest and lower your spine, one vertebra at a time, with your tail bone last.

Uddiyana

In Sanskrit, 'Uddiyana' means 'flying up'. In this exercise the air is drawn up from the lower abdomen and moves under the ribcage toward the head. This movement tones the abdominal organs, increases the gastric juices and eliminates toxins in the digestive tract. It is a wonderful way to exercise the muscles of the stomach, thereby making it flatter.

Kneel down on all fours. Keep your spine straight and place your hands and feet in a direct line. Inhale through your nose and exhale through your mouth until all the breath is out of your lungs.

Pull the stomach muscles up and curve your spine slightly. Without taking a breath, contract and release the muscles to massage the internal organs. When you tire, inhale and exhale normally for a few breaths. Repeat the whole exercise up to 20 times.

Ultimate Twist

These two twists are classic positions to increase circulation in the spine and the abdominal organs, especially the liver and spleen. Twists cleanse and purify the system and are essential to the digestive system. Elimination is regulated, the kidneys are toned, and the blood circulation releases toxins that build up in the internal organs. When you are practicing twists you will find that every time you begin the pose it will be a different experience. As the flexibility of your spine increases you will be able to twist even further. Sluggishness will be replaced by higher energy levels and you will experience a feeling of youthfulness.

Sit with knees together and feet flat on the ground. Place your right elbow on the outside of your left knee and put your left hand on the floor in the opposite direction to your feet. Push against your knee and look over your left shoulder. Keeping your chin level and breathing normally, continue to stretch around. Hold for as long as you can. Repeat on the other side.

Sit with your left leg over your right leg. Take your right hand to the left knee and twist, looking as far over your left shoulder as possible. Place your left hand on the floor in line with your left leg. Breathe normally and continue to twist. Repeat on the other side.

Leg Pull

The Leg Pull increases the flexibility of the hamstrings and tones muscle in the knees and legs. It also tones the spine and massages the abdominal wall; blood flows around the navel and rejuvenates the genital organs. Never lift the knee that is resting on the floor – if there is too much of a pull on the kneecap do not extend your chin all the way to your knee.

1

Sit with both legs extended in front. Bend your left knee and bring your heel to your hip. Place your fingertips on the floor on either side of your body. Breathe normally.

2

Bend your right knee and clasp your first two fingers around your big toe. Flex your thumb and right foot and prepare for the stretch.

3

Keeping your spine straight, inhale and stretch the leg up in front of you. Hold your ankle and pull your leg towards you. Breathing slowly and evenly, hold for 20 seconds. If you can, place your chin and forehead to the leg. Repeat on the other side.

Sitting Balance

The Sitting Balance is an excellent test for checking your alignment – you will be unable to carry out this exercise if your spine is not in the correct position. Imagine your spine to be a group of children's building blocks; if you do not place each block evenly on to the next the whole building will come tumbling down. By the same token, if you do not lift your spine upright you will keep rolling back down to the floor. Concentrate on your stomach muscles because it is equally important to pull them in at the same time as you lift your spine.

2

Still sitting upright, bring your legs up to form an exact right-angle with the body.

1

Sit upright and bring your knees up with your feet flat on the floor. Clasp your elbows under your knees. Keep your spine straight and breathe normally.

4

Shift your hands up your legs and take hold of your ankles. Pull your head toward your knees, keeping your spine straight and pulling your stomach muscles in. Breathe normally and hold for at least 5 seconds.

Straighten both legs up in front of you and hold the position absolutely still for at least 5 seconds, breathing normally.

1

Lie on your stomach and lift your legs up behind you. Hold on to your ankles and point your toes. Place your chin and nose on the floor. Breathe normally.

The Bow

This exercise is called the Bow because of the beautiful bow shape that the spine creates. The back muscles and internal organs are massaged and the latter invigorated. Because of the position of the abdomen, this asana helps to cure digestive and bowel disorders such as gastroenteritis and constipation. It also stimulates the appetite, aids digestion and reduces fat along the stomach and middle of the back. As a result of the increased suppleness it gives to the spine every cell in the body is rejuvenated and revitalized, giving you renewed vitality and a more youthful appearance.

2

Inhale and lift your body up in one movement. Balance on your hip bones and keep stretching upward, trying to get your head in line with your feet. Breathe deeply and hold for as long as you can.

The Camel

The Camel tones the entire spine as well as every muscle group in the body, building strength in the lower back and alleviating back ailments, especially sciatica and slipped discs. It is also a wonderful stretch for the face and neck – the increased circulation helps to prevent the signs of ageing. Every time you do this exercise, feel your body giving way into the stretch and relax and open the throat and chest; do not allow any weight into the thighs or leg muscles. Always push upward from the hips to increase the intensity of the back stretch and breathe deeply throughout. If you experience a sharp pain in the lower back, stop immediately and relax in Step 3. A dull pain means you are using muscles around the spine that need toning.

Kneel down, spine straight and hips directly above your knees. Hold on to your elbows behind your lower back. Inhale, push your hips forward and drop your head back. Breathe normally.

Continuing to push your hips forward, take your hands to your heels. Open your chest and throat and relax your face, neck and shoulders. Say 'Aah' to check that your facial muscles are relaxed. Breathe normally and hold for as long as possible.

To release the spine, reverse the position by relaxing your head down to the floor with your palms facing up. Breathe normally and repeat the exercise.

The Rabbit

The Rabbit allows fresh oxygen into the blood supply, which stimulates and invigorates the brain cells. The upside-down position of the head has a beneficial effect on the pituitary gland and thyroid. It wards off senility, clarifies the mind, regulates the metabolism and strengthens the immune system. It also has a calming effect on the nervous system. A preliminary exercise to the Head Stand (opposite), the Rabbit improves the elasticity and mobility of the spine.

2

Inhale and as you exhale curl your spine and place your forehead on the floor as close as you can to your knees. Breathe normally.

3

Roll on to the top of your head. Straighten your elbows and raise your hips. Breathe deeply and hold for 20 seconds. Return to Step 1 and repeat the exercise.

1

Kneel on the floor, toes tucked under your haunches. Clasp your hands to your heels and sit up tall. Breathe normally.

Head Stand

1

Kneel on the floor. Interlock your fingers, cross your thumbs and place your arms on the floor. Breathe normally.

The Head Stand is called the king of all yoga asanas because it stimulates the pituitary and pineal glands. These are the glands that control the brain, the seat of all wisdom, intelligence, discrimination and reasoning power. Without a healthy brain you cannot function. The inverted position of the Head Stand allows the blood to flow freely to the brain and feeds the brain cells with fresh oxygen. It gives you clarity of mind and wards off senility as you age. The brain also controls the entire nervous system and during the practice of the Head Stand all the nerves and cells are being rejuvenated. Health and vitality are restored and when you practice it on a regular basis you will develop the body, discipline the mind and broaden the spirit.

2

Making sure your elbows are directly under your shoulder blades, place the top of your head down on the floor just in front of your hands.

3

Tuck your toes under and spring up onto your toes with your legs straight. Walk your feet toward your head until your spine is straight.

▶

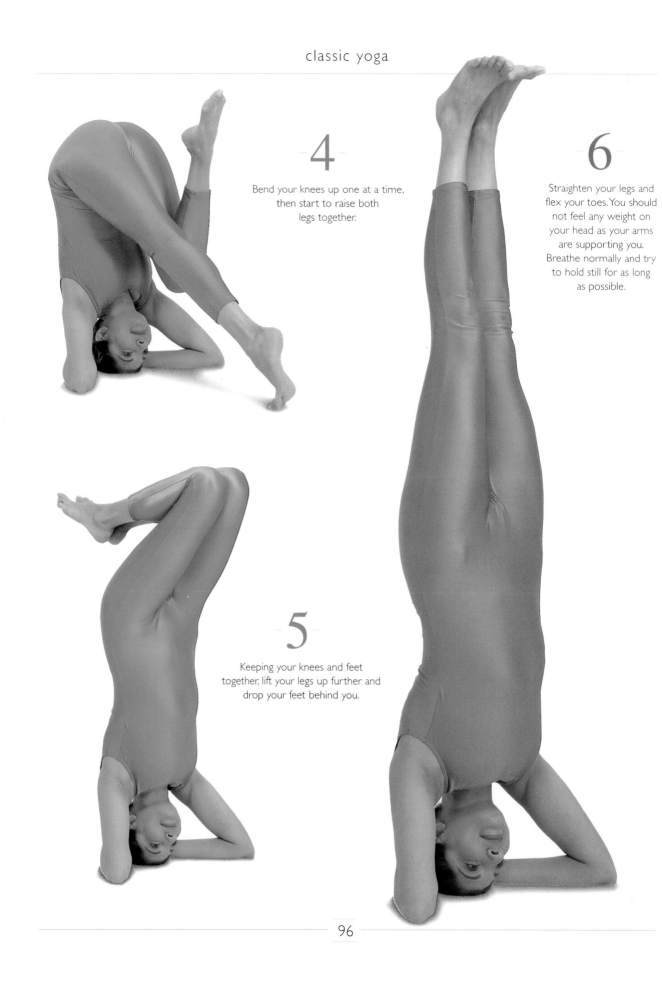

4

Bend your knees up one at a time, then start to raise both legs together.

5

Keeping your knees and feet together, lift your legs up further and drop your feet behind you.

6

Straighten your legs and flex your toes. You should not feel any weight on your head as your arms are supporting you. Breathe normally and try to hold still for as long as possible.

7

Open your legs to second position, keeping your feet flexed. Hold for 10 seconds.

8

Bend your knees at a right angle.

9

Slowly bring your knees forward, curving your spine, and return to the floor. Stay in this position for 10 seconds. If you come up suddenly you will feel dizzy.

Total Stretch

This stretch is very controversial – some people find it excruciating, while others feel it to be the most marvellous of all the classic stretches. The truth is that the more flexible you are the easier the pose. It stretches every muscle in the thighs, knees and ankles, as well the entire spine. If you feel any pain in your back, place a pillow under the small of the back and open your chest. If you feel your knees are strained place a small pillow under the back of your knees. The most important thing to remember is to relax in the position. Breathe deeply and evenly and feel the chest and hips open.

Sit upright and bring your knees together. Spread your feet and rest them either side of your hips, with your buttocks on the floor. Place your palms facing forward on your feet.

Drop your body back down, taking your weight on your elbows, and feel the stretch in your legs and abdomen.

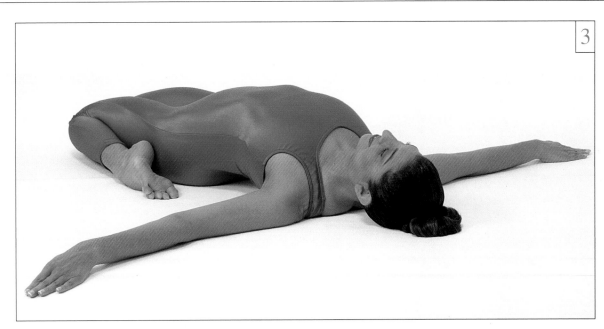

Lie back flat on the floor with your arms stretched out to the sides.

Clasp your elbows. Continue to breathe deeply and relax the entire body and mind. Try to hold this position for as long as possible – with practice you will be able to sustain it for 10–15 minutes.

yoga to relieve
stress

The aim of yoga is to unify the entire system through breathing techniques, gentle exercise and mind control. This combination of practices produces an inner calm and tranquility that goes deep into the mind and body. The result is a feeling of peace and harmony that translates in the way you think and react to certain situations. When you are relaxed and in control of your thoughts and emotions you are better able to cope with even the hardest problems. Most people panic when faced with difficulties and this increases stress levels immediately. Simply learning to breathe from the diaphragm acts as a natural tranquilizer that calms the nervous system instantly. In addition, the gentle movement and deep stretching of yoga improves the circulation and releases tension in the muscle groups. Another aspect of yoga is the visualisation and meditation techniques, which help to train and focus the mind. Although there are five different schools of yoga, all concentrate on the philosophy of reaching spiritual enlightenment through uniting mind and body. Yoga transforms people's lives by teaching them a new way of thinking and viewing the world, providing an anchor in an increasingly frenetic age.

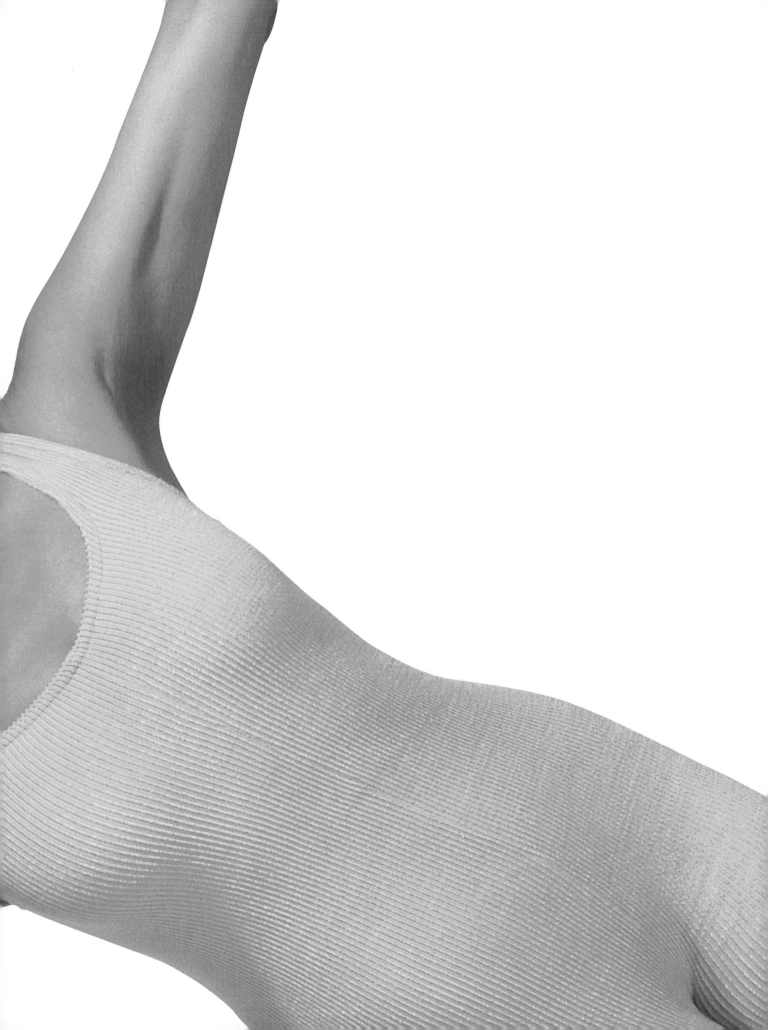

Energy Boosters

People who suffer from stress complain of fatigue, depression and generally feeling unwell. They usually lead sedentary lives with little exercise and seem to have no joy in anything they do; lack of energy affects their mental health and erodes their self-esteem. Acidic foods, diets containing stimulants, and medication also deplete the body of energy. Yoga exercise is the best way to boost the body by releasing tension in the muscles as well as improving blood circulation and lymphatic drainage. Deep breathing, combined with stretching, increases the oxygen in the system and rejuvenates all body cells, giving you more energy. When stress is deeply rooted in the muscle groups, any jarring movements can cause injury. Yoga, with its gentle approach, will slowly ease the stress in the body while increasing stamina and strength. Stress can also cause stiffness in the ligaments and joints, and bending forward, backward and sideways can increase your body's flexibility and energy flow. Twisting movements release toxins from the organs, and inverted positions soothe the nervous system. Yoga exercises also lubricate the joints and arteries and build muscle tone as you age. In this chapter I have developed a gentle, easy, safe exercise program for people of all ages to release tension, increase energy levels and tone the body. There are also shorter energy boosters for home, work and travel to lift your spirits and rejuvenate you.

Forward Stretch

Stretching forward lengthens the spine and helps to calm the nervous system. It opens out the hips and tones up the leg muscles. It is important to lift the muscles above the knees to increase your balance and to enable you to grip the floor with your toes. Always extend your body from the base of your spine while you tighten your abdominal muscles. Some people can feel slightly dizzy because of the increased oxygen in the system, but it passes quickly as you learn to deepen your breathing. As you push your elbows back you will open your chest and release any tension in the neck, shoulders and upper back. In the final position try to concentrate on one point on the floor and keep your back flat in a straight line from the neck to the tail bone.

Stand up straight with your feet 1–1.2m (3–4ft) apart and toes pointing forward. ▸ Place your hands on your waist and open out your chest. Inhale deeply and look upward, drawing the elbows toward each other. ▸ Lean forward and point your chin, stretching from the hips and tailbone to straighten the spine. ▸ As you continue to inhale, pause with your back straight and your hips, shoulders and head at a 90° angle. Exhale and hold this position for a few seconds while you breathe normally. ▸ Inhale again and continue stretching downward, exhaling when you have reached as far as you can. Breathe normally and hold this position for 10 seconds. As you deepen your breaths, try to stretch even further without forcing or jerking your body.

When you reach the final position, continue with the exercise on pages 106–7.

Head to Knee Side Twist

This exercise increases your spine's flexibility, releases toxins from your internal organs and helps back ailments such as sciatica and lumbago. When you take your head forward it helps to soothe your nerves, making you feel calm and relaxed. Suppleness of the spine is essential for good circulation and this exercise combined with deep breathing increases the blood flow through the arteries to boost your energy. When you start to twist, try to turn as far as you can. The final position releases any stiffness you are experiencing in the lower back, neck and shoulders, and also helps to build muscle strength so that you can sit and stand tall.

Continuing from the previous exercise, inhale deeply and as you exhale reach down to your feet, clasping your hands around your ankles. Inhale and exhale deeply for a few seconds to increase the stretch. ▶ Now take both of your hands over to the right ankle. If you cannot reach your ankle, take your hands down your right leg as far as you can. ▶ Inhale and take your right arm out to the side in a straight line. ▶ Continue to inhale as you start to twist your body around to the back. ▶ Look over your right shoulder and continue to twist as far as possible. Exhale and hold this final position for 10 seconds. Return to the start position and repeat the exercise on the other side.

Spinal Stretch

This spinal stretch increases your blood circulation and the flow of oxygen to the brain, helping to relieve tension. It also tones and increases the flexibility of the hamstrings, hips and spine and tones the leg muscles. As you take your arms over your head your breathing pattern becomes shallower, so you have to breathe more deeply to sustain an even pattern. This increase in breathing rejuvenates the body's cells and helps to purify the internal organs. You will experience a tingling sensation in your toes and fingertips as your energy flow is increased. Also your face will glow when you can hold the final position for some time.

Stand upright with your feet slightly apart, then take hold of your ankles and gently stretch down toward your legs. ▶ Cross your arms, holding onto your elbows. Inhale deeply and pull in your abdominal muscles as you begin to stretch your arms over your head. ▶ Keep your spine straight and push your hips back behind you. To maintain your balance, shift your weight back onto your heels and grip the floor with your toes. ▶ Holding your stomach muscles taut, bring your arms up to your head with your head, neck, shoulders and hips in a straight line. Exhale and breathe deeply, holding this position for 30 seconds. You will feel energized and calmer as you breathe more deeply. To release the stretch, relax your spine and drop your head down toward your feet. Hold for a few seconds, then slowly raise yourself upright.

Deep Bend I

This bending posture promotes total body health because it allows the energy to flow through the entire system. Not only does the exercise soothe the brain but harmful toxins are also eliminated from the body's organs as the head bends forward. The spine becomes more flexible and supple, which gives you a feeling of elation. This posture also stimulates the sciatic nerve and strengthens the muscles of the lower back. Always gently lengthen the spine forward – never force your body or jerk into the pose. Breathe deeply as you relax forward, eventually trying to stretch out your entire spine as you clasp your ankles.

Stand up straight and bring your feet together, then lean down and hold onto your ankles with both hands, keeping your elbows straight. ▸ Pulling your tummy muscles in, inhale deeply, bend your elbows and slowly stretch your forehead toward your knees. ▸ Exhale and pull your head further down. ▸ Breathing deeply and slowly, lengthen your spine as you try to touch your knees with your forehead. Hold the position for 30 seconds. Do not become discouraged if you cannot reach down very far. With continued practice you will be amazed at how far down you can reach.

Think of your spine as circles of energy around the vertebrae and not a solid mass. This will help the way you approach this position as you ease softly and gently down.

Perfect Posture

It is vital to understand good body alignment and to learn how to sit and stand in perfect posture. Bad posture leads to back ailments, a negative mental outlook and depleted energies. When you are standing and sitting correctly you can breathe properly to your full lung capacity. Most people with bad posture never experience the joy of feeling full of vitality. Stretching in perfect posture aligns and balances the muscles and corrects the tilt of the pelvis. It allows the spine to stay erect so that the body's energy flows freely. By stretching your arms over your head you open out your chest and your hips are free, giving more space for the internal organs to function properly.

Stand upright with feet together and big toes touching and try to balance. Distribute your weight evenly between your heels and toes and grip the floor with your toes. Place your hands on your ankles with your head tucked in. ▸ Inhale deeply, straighten your arms and pull up halfway. ▸ Then bring your arms out in front of you close to your ears, tightening your tummy and buttock muscles. ▸ Keep stretching your arms outward with a straight spine as you stand up. ▸ Lift your arms above your head, exhale and breathe normally. Keep your head lifted, your neck extended and your breastbone stretched upward. Then lift your diaphragm, rib cage and abdomen, and tuck in your tail bone; tighten your leg muscles. Release your arms down and stand for 30 seconds, drawing your energies into yourself.

As you stretch up do not hyper-extend your knees by pushing them backward, but lift the muscles above your knees.

Deep Bend II

Flexible hip joints help to correct any pelvic imbalance and improve mobility as we get older. This stretch looks simple to do, but it really is a dynamic movement which creates poise and confidence. Keeping your spine upright in perfect alignment while you bend helps you breathe more deeply, but holding the pose can be quite strenous. As you lunge sideways, make sure your knee does not extend right over your foot as this can cause knee strain. The movement should create a 90° angle from the upper body to the back of the knee and heel.

Stand upright with your feet 1.2m (4ft) apart, your toes pointing forward and both hands on your waist. Turn your left foot to the left, keeping the instep of the right foot in line with the left heel. Place your left hand on your left leg with your fingertips on the inner thigh above the knee. Keep your spine straight and hips square, and remember to breathe deeply and evenly throughout the exercise. ▸ Bend your left knee to turn the thigh and hip joints. If the knee moves beyond the foot, take the right leg out further to create a 90° angle. ▸ Now extend the lunge further by pushing the pubic bone down toward the floor, keeping the right leg straight. Push the right foot down toward the floor, tightening the muscle above the knee. Keep your pelvis straight and your breastbone lifted. Enjoy the elation of the stretch, while holding for 10 seconds or more. To release the pose return to the start position and repeat the exercise on the other side.

Cat Stretch

This is a wonderful exercise to relieve all the tension that accumulates in the spine. It also helps to calm the brain and relaxes the neck and shoulders. If you suffer from headaches and backaches caused by stress, you will find that if you place your head down on the floor in this curved position it will help to alleviate the pain. Combined with deep breathing, this exercise soothes your central nervous system and helps you to restore harmony and balance to your life. It slows down your pulse rate and gives you time to escape from any mental anxieties by relaxing the brain so that you find inner calm.

Begin by kneeling down on all fours on the floor and stretch your arms out in front of you. ▸ Inhale deeply and begin to drop your hips back toward your heels. ▸ Exhale and push your hips all the way down so that your chest rests on your knees, bending your elbows and dropping your head forward to the floor. ▸ Breathing in and out deeply, slide your arms back toward your heels. Curl your spine and relax down onto your forehead, sliding your hands back beyond your heels with your palms facing up. Hold until you feel totally relaxed. Do this exercise to rejuvenate yourself if you are feeling tired or lethargic, or use it to shut yourself off from the rest of the world. You can drift into peaceful sleep by turning to one side and rolling over to stretch out your legs.

Home:
Body Rolls

When your body stiffens and tenses with stress your spine feels locked. Your normal mobility is blocked and you experience aches and pains throughout your body. The best exercise to relieve this stress is body rolls, as the movements release tension and boost energy levels. Combined with correct breathing the exercise increases your vitality and improves your circulation. While you are breathing deeply and moving your body in a circle the fresh oxygen moving through your body revitalizes, cleanses and purifies the internal organs. Some people feel dizzy in this pose because they have too many toxins in their body. Body rolls are easy to do at home, improve your balance, and encourage a sense of wellbeing.

Stand up straight with your feet pointing forward 1m (3ft) apart. Take your hands to your waist and open out your chest. ▸ Inhale and stretch your body to the right, keeping your knees straight. Do not drop your head but keep it in line with your neck. ▸ Still inhaling, push your hips forward and extend your head backward, relaxing your neck and shoulders. ▸ Exhale and stretch your body to the left. ▸ Now flatten your spine and turn your body toward the floor, looking downward. ▸ Still exhaling, move forward between your legs and extend down toward the floor. Inhale and return to the start position. Repeat the exercise on the other side. Some people have more tension and stiffness than others, so continue the rolls until you feel your body starting to rejuvenate with energy.

Work:
Slow Stretching

Many people spend their working day slouched over a desk and consequently suffer from backache, fatigue, boredom and a sense of failure if they cannot cope with their workload. The best way to change these reactions is to boost the energy levels and calm the nervous system. Tension and stress stay in your body until they are consciously removed. If left, your body will seize up and your spine will become immobile. The way to avoid these symptoms is to find a suitable place in your office to do this exercise to release tension and restore mental harmony. Stretching up releases muscular tension in the neck and shoulders and bending forward soothes and revitalizes the nervous system.

Stand up straight with feet together, inhale deeply and throw your arms above your head with palms facing. Keep your shoulders down and your head centered between your arms. Exhale and hold briefly. ▶ Cross your arms, hold onto your elbows and push your elbows behind your ears. ▶ Inhale and as you exhale stretch over to the left from the waist with hips and feet forward. Breathe normally and hold briefly. Inhale and return to the center again. ▶ Exhale and stretch over to the right in the same way. Breathe normally. ▶ Then, with your back straight, extend your spine forward. ▶ Relax down by breathing more deeply and bring your head to your knees. Close your eyes, holding for 10 seconds. Inhale and return to the start position. Repeat the exercise.

Travel:
Hands and Feet

When you have to sit still for a long period while travelling on a plane, coach or train, your body stiffens up and you begin to feel lethargic and tired. Because you are in a confined space it is difficult to move and stretch your aching muscles without causing disturbance to the other passengers. This exercise will help to release any tension you may suffer in the sciatic nerves in your back and will also improve your blood circulation while you are forced to remain static. Gently moving your feet will alleviate any numbness or the 'pins and needles' that many people experience when they have to sit in a cramped position for any length of time.

While you are seated, extend your legs forward and flex your toes upward. (If space is too limited to do this, you can perform the exercise in the normal sitting position.) ▸ Point your toes and move both feet in a circle, first to the right and then to the left. ▸ Still pointing your toes, cross your ankles, roll onto your left hip and twist as far as you can. ▸ Move back to the center and roll onto your right hip, twisting as far as you can. ▸ Release your feet and sit up straight, taking your arms over your head with your elbows bent. Now shake your arms and hands to release any tension and improve your circulation. ▸ Keep shaking both arms around your body until your hands come down to your hips. Repeat the exercise as necessary.

Art of Relaxation

Learning to soothe your nerves and calm your nervous system is the aim of the exercises in this chapter. Stress gets locked in the physical body and the goal is to release this muscular tension gently through a series of flowing movements. Stress can cause stiffness, especially in the neck, shoulders and lower back, leading to bad posture. Tension and stress are held in the body unconsciously and the moment people are made aware of their physical condition they will instinctively try to relax and find balance, as this is the natural state. Yoga is ideal for relaxation because it teaches you to shut yourself off from the rest of the world and go into the deeper realms of your mind to find lasting inner peace. When you relax deeply your nerve endings are rejuvenated and your nervous system functions better. The purpose of the exercises in the first part of this chapter is to release tension in specific muscle groups. The inverted postures, such as the modified shoulder stand, will calm the nervous system. Whenever the head drops forward, a sudden feeling of calm will prevail. In the dead man's pose your body metabolism slows down. Make sure you are in a warm, quiet room wearing unrestricted clothing when you exercise. By doing these exercises you will bring peace to your body and mind at will.

Shoulder Shrugs and Rolls

When people are very stressed and wound up, tension accumulates in the body, especially in the neck and shoulders. The only way to release this stiffness is to exaggerate the movement between the neck and shoulders while breathing deeply and evenly. When you do this exercise it is very important to keep your head straight and in correct alignment to your back and neck. As you inhale, focus your attention on the stiffness in your muscles and when you exhale imagine all the muscular tension leaving your body. Every person is different and will hold tension in certain weak spots. Visualize and concentrate on these areas and you will be amazed at how quickly you can feel relaxed.

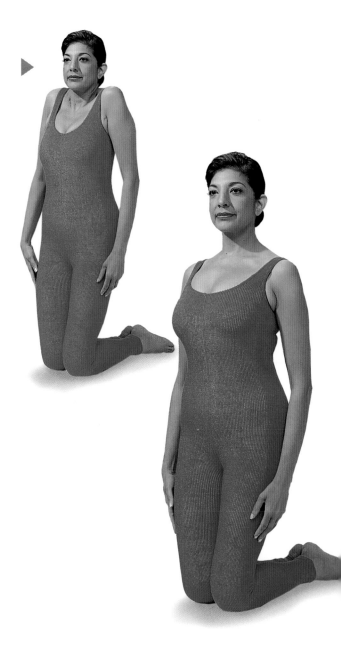

Kneeling on the floor, inhale and take your shoulders up high toward your ears. ▸ As you exhale drop your shoulders down and push your shoulder blades together, opening out your chest. Repeat a few times until the stiffness starts to leave your body. Breathe deeply to help shift the tightness. ▸ Now inhale and repeat the shoulder shrug. ▸ As you exhale, move your shoulders back in a circular motion. ▸ To repeat the exercise, inhale and take your shoulders forward and up, then exhale as you take them back and down. Keep all your movements fluid and graceful. Return to the start position. As you exercise, keep still, concentrating on your neck and shoulders.

127

Back Roll

When you really need to relax this back roll releases any stress and strain from the tail bone of the spine right up to the top of the neck. By taking your legs over your head you calm the nervous system and soothe the nerves. If you suffer from backache this is the easiest and safest exercise to relieve any pain. Also, when your body is feeling exhausted and needs a quick boost, this exercise combined with some deep breathing rejuvenates your entire system. You may find it hard in the beginning to take your legs right over your head, but just let the force of your natural body weight allow your legs and spine to roll over gently. At first you may need to push your palms down to the floor to help you roll over, but with practice you will soon realize that a supple spine is the main key to success.

Lie down on the floor with legs outstretched and arms at your side. Breathe deeply and evenly and feel your whole body relaxing. Draw your feet back, cross your ankles and place your palms upward, keeping your eyes closed. ▸ Bring your knees toward your chest and hold onto your toes, keeping your elbows straight. ▸ Inhale and slowly bring your knees and thighs down to your chest. ▸ Pull your tummy muscles in and start to take your legs over your head. ▸ Roll over completely and stretch your spine as far as possible. Keep your knees as close to your ears as possible and relax your neck and shoulder muscles. Exhale, and breathe deeply in this position, holding for at least 30 seconds. Repeat the exercise a few times until your body feels totally calm and relaxed.

Modified Shoulder Stand

The shoulder stand helps to regulate your metabolism and balance your hormones. People who suffer regularly from stress often experience mood swings and weight fluctuations. This exercise helps to stabilize your temperament and weight and calms your mind. Two of the most important glands in the body are the pituitary and thyroid. According to the yogic texts, locking your chin into your chest stimulates your thyroid gland to help it function normally. When you are inverted with your legs above your head the blood flows downward to all your organs, replenishing and oxygenating the cells. This increased blood flow rejuvenates and relaxes your whole body.

Lie on the floor, legs outstretched and arms at your side. Bring your knees up, put your feet on the floor and place your palms facing down. ▸ Inhale deeply, pushing your palms down, while bringing your knees up to your chest. ▸ Keep pushing your palms down and lift your spine off the floor. ▸ Take your hands to your waist to support your back and lift your legs up. Lock your chin into your chest. Exhale, and breathe normally while holding this position. Try to hold still for 30–60 seconds. To come down, inhale, and while exhaling slowly lower your back and legs to the floor. Keep breathing deeply and evenly. If you experience any back discomfort do the Back Roll (pages 128–9).

Knee Twist

This simple knee twist exercise helps to strengthen the spine as well as releasing toxins from the system. The more flexible your spine is, the more you will be able to twist around. It is very important to sit upright to lift your spine correctly. Some people who have weak backs might feel a dull pain in the lumbar region. As you build up these muscles you will feel uncomfortable if you are not sitting upright. The intensity of the twist is felt when the spine is the only part of the body that is moving as the hips stay immobile and in line. The most wonderful thing about twists is that there is no final position. Challenge yourself and try to twist even further every time you do this exercise.

Start the twist sitting on the floor with your legs outstretched in front of you. Sitting up as tall as possible, flex your feet upward. ▸ Bend your left knee and bring your foot in as close as possible, holding onto your leg with both hands. Make sure you do not collapse your spine at this time. If you feel your back caving in, place your foot further out. ▸ With your right arm, hold onto your left leg with your right elbow in front of your knee for a tighter grip. ▸ Take your left hand and place it on your lower back with your palm facing up. Inhale and twist as far as possible, looking over your left shoulder. Exhale and breathe normally as you deepen the twist. To release the spine, gradually unwind and return to the front, still holding your leg, and then return to the start position. Repeat the exercise on the other side, and then do twice on each side.

Dead Man's Pose

Relaxing is a technique that needs to be learned in order to maximize your capability for relaxation at will. Yoga is ideal because it allows your mind to shut out useless thoughts and relax the brain at a deeper level. This achieves stillness of the mind which helps to clarify thoughts and emotions. This exercise can rejuvenate your energy by relaxing every body nerve, and it can help cure insomnia. Find a quiet place and, because your body temperature will drop, make sure you feel warm and comfortable.

Lie flat on the floor, knees up and arms at your side. If you wish to, you can put a small pillow under your head. Breathe deeply and evenly through your nose, mouth closed. Relax your face until you feel calm. ▸ Slowly relax your legs down onto the floor. ▸ Sink your tail bone into the floor, taking your arms out at your sides with palms facing upward. Leave your feet apart and your throat open. Keep breathing deeply and slowly. Now concentrate on each muscle group, beginning with the tummy, buttocks, thighs, knees, ankles, feet and toes. Inhale and tighten each section. Hold for 5 seconds. Exhale and release. Then work on the back, arms and hands. Tighten your fists to release tension. Now do your neck. Inhale, taking your shoulders up to your ears. Exhale and release. Repeat. Take your head from side to side and then let it drop. Relax your face. Keep still for 5–15 minutes. ▸ To release, turn to one side, bringing your knees into your chest. Rest until you feel like getting up.

Home:
Knee Twists

These simple knee twists are excellent to release tension throughout the body. As you ease your hips from side to side you can sometimes feel the muscles click into place to realign the spine. The movement also gives relief for backache. The blood supply to the discs and nerves is boosted, and the spine becomes toned. To twist laterally with safety, the pelvis should be the only region that moves; twisting from the shoulders and ribs can strain the lower back. Keep the movement graceful and fluid and use the tummy muscles to help control the action of twisting from one side to the other.

Start the exercise lying flat on the floor with your legs outstretched and your arms at your sides. Inhale and bring your knees toward your chest, stretching your arms to the sides with palms facing downward in line with the shoulders, as in position 3. Exhale and keep your neck and head in line with your spine. Inhale and as you exhale take your knees down to the floor on the left, while twisting your head in the opposite direction. ▸ Inhale and bring your knees and head gradually back to the center. ▸ Exhale and take your head to the left as you twist your knees to the right. Inhale and return your knees and head to the center. Exhale. Repeat the exercise from side to side until you feel that all your tension has been released and you are totally relaxed. Return to Dead Man's Pose position 3 and 4 (pages 134–5).

Work:
Eyes, Jaw and Neck

Though space is often limited in the workplace, it is still important to release any stress that builds up during the day due to the pressures at work. The first tension spots are the eyes, jaw, neck and shoulders, and this exercise is the most effective way of releasing all the stiffness in these areas quickly. You will feel relieved immediately and be able to face the rest of the day knowing that you have an instant solution if the problem reoccurs. During the exercise, breathe as deeply as possible to help movement and calm the nervous system.

Sit on a chair or on the floor and cross your legs at the ankles. Sit up tall and clasp your hands behind your neck. Open out your elbows in line with your shoulders and push your shoulder blades down. ▶ Inhale deeply and slowly bring your elbows together. Exhale and return your elbows to position 1. Remember to keep your head straight in line with your neck and shoulders. Repeat. ▶ Now look upward as high as possible without tilting backward. Inhale, and bring your elbows together as before. Drop your head back and as you exhale open the elbows as much as possible. Open your mouth to release your jaw, and close. Repeat this jaw action twice and return to position 1. Repeat this section. Now release your arms and continue to sit upright. ▶ Rub your hands together to generate heat and blow into your palms. ▶ Place both palms over your eyes. This soothes the eyes and helps reduce pounding headaches. Breathe deeply and hold for as long as you can.

Travel:
Hands and Feet

Whenever you sit still in one place for a length of time, as happens in travelling, your circulation becomes blocked. Also, some people feel panicky when they are confined to a small place where they cannot move around freely, and indeed many people have a real fear of travelling. Trying to keep calm and relaxed is the best solution to these insecurities. Breathing from your diaphragm acts as a natural tranquilizer to your nervous system, so the deeper you breathe the calmer your mind will become. During these stressful travel situations, start to lengthen your breaths and soon you will be taking deep breaths naturally.

Start by sitting upright in your plane or train seat or when you are taking a break from driving. Take your left hand around the back of your neck and open out your elbow. ▶ Inhale and twist your neck and head to the right, bringing your elbow down into your chest to increase the stretch. Exhale, and return to position 1. Repeat 2–3 times. Now take your right hand around the back of the neck and repeat the exercise 2–3 times. ▶ Return to position 1 and take your right hand to hold your elbow behind your head. Stretch both elbows back. Breathe normally, and repeat on the other side.
▶ Now clasp both elbows with your hands over your head and take them back behind your ears. Breathe normally and hold for 5–10 seconds.
▶ Relax forward, placing your forehead down on your knees or table. Relax deeply, breathing evenly, and feel the stress leave your spine.

Meditation and Visualization

Meditation is a skill that clarifies and focuses the mind. Mastery over the mind is achieved through yoga meditation because it teaches you to concentrate on one subject in the first stage and calm your mind in the second. Mental breakdowns caused by stress can be greatly alleviated. Through meditation a person can observe their symptoms and reactions objectively, and change their attitudes toward their ailment. Meditating will bring them back to harmony and restore the balance that was lost. The yoga student can use meditation for practical purposes or move ahead into the deeper realms of the mind to discover universal truths and spiritual bliss. We begin with breathing exercises to calm the mind, as deep breathing acts as a natural tranquilizer. The meditation poses are all sitting positions to keep your spine erect. The true position is the lotus, because your tail bone nearly touches the floor, allowing the energy to move freely through the body's energy centers to the crown chakra in the head to connect with cosmic energy. Visualization is another technique to help train your mind for meditation. To start visualizing, sit in a meditation pose and think of a happy experience when you were close to nature. Observe your surroundings, emotions and reactions to the environment to stop your mind wandering.

Breathing

Learning how to control your breathing is fundamental to training and controlling your mind. In this exercise we learn how to contract and release the abdominal muscles to regulate the flow of *prana*, or energy. Because of these movements the abdominal organs are toned and internally massaged and the gastric juices are stimulated, which aids digestion. The exercise helps to eliminate toxins in the digestive tract as well as regulating the bowel. The contraction and release action helps to trim excess fat from the stomach and flatten the tummy. It is always best to do this *bandha* or breathing technique on an empty stomach. Allow 4–6 hours after eating a heavy meal, but a light beverage such as tea can be taken 30 minutes before. The more you do this exercise, the more you will notice the benefits. At first you might find it difficult to regulate your breathing correctly, but with practice you will understand why this breathing technique is taught to maintain good body health.

Start the exercise kneeling on the floor with your hands directly in line with your knees. Inhale deeply and then exhale quickly through your nose so that air is forced from your lungs in a rush. ▸ When all your breath is totally released, hold your breath and contract your abdominal muscles upward behind your rib cage toward your spine. Hold for 5 seconds. ▸ Still holding your breath, release your muscles and rib cage. Hold for 5 seconds. ▸ Inhale again and drop your spine down. Exhale and breathe normally. Repeat the whole exercise twice and build up to 10 times or more.

Pranayama

It is important to learn how to breathe properly, so set aside a regular time in a comfortable, airy space each day to practice *pranayama* techniques. *Pranayama* is the science of breath control. This particular breathing exercise is a simple one and helps you understand how to regulate your breathing pattern. At first you might find it difficult to lengthen your breath and exhale in a controlled way. Look at your posture, your breathing rhythm, and the way in which you breathe. When you exhale, your ribcage should expand forward and sideways, but the area below your shoulder blades and armpits should expand only forward. The thumb and finger contact signifies the symbol of knowledge. The thumb is the universal soul and the index finger the individual soul; together they form the seal of wisdom.

Sit cross-legged, hands on the floor, with a straight spine and your head in line with your neck. Relax your muscles, especially in your face. Close your eyes to calm your mind. Breathe deeply and evenly. Take your thumb and index finger together. Inhale deeply through your nose and drop your head back without moving your spine. ▶ Open your mouth slightly and form the letter 'O'. ▶ Slowly exhale through your mouth as you drop your head until your chin rests on your chest. ▶ Do not cave in your chest or spine, and exhale evenly. The longer you exhale the better, so when you are practiced in the technique, exhale for 5 seconds, building up to 10 seconds. Repeat at least 5 times.

Pranayama
(nostril breathing)

Alternate nostril breathing is an advanced breathing technique. The energies of the body, whether male or female, have both masculine and feminine properties. The right side signifies the masculine energies, while the left side is the feminine. Alternate nostril breathing harmonizes these energies to restore balance to mind and body. The even breathing strengthens your nerves and encourages a balanced temperament and sound mind. Keep your breaths long, steady and deep. If you cannot maintain an even breathing rhythm, stop immediately in case you strain your lungs and diaphragm, and check your technique.

Sit crosslegged on the floor. Lift your spine up, but keep your shoulders down. Keep the thumb and index finger together on your left hand and rest it on your left knee. Bend your three main fingers into your right palm, but stretch up your thumb and little finger. Block your left nostril with your little finger and breathe deeply through your right nostril. Close your eyes, relaxing your face and body muscles. Inhale for 5 seconds and exhale for 5 seconds. Repeat 10 times on the right nostril and then block the right nostril with your thumb and repeat 10 times on the left. ▸ Then inhale from the right for 5 seconds, hold your breath for 3, blocking your nostril with your thumb, and exhale through the left for 5 seconds. ▸ Inhale from the left nostril for 5 seconds, hold for 3, and exhale through the right for 5 seconds. Repeat the exercise at least 10 times.

Chakras and Candle Gazing

'Chakra' is a Sanskrit word meaning 'wheels' that radiate energy in a circular pattern through the spine's vital centers. Just as antennae pick up radio waves and turn them into sound, chakras pick up on cosmic vibrations and distribute them through the body's energy centers. To maintain good health it is vital to keep the centers generating equal energy through the body. If a chakra is blocked with too much or too little energy the body becomes unbalanced. Acupuncture uses needles placed in the energy centers to restore balance, and in yoga we learn *pranayama* (breath control) to ensure that the correct energy flows evenly through the body. Candle gazing (see page 153), a technique to train the mind to focus on one thought, helps to restore harmony to the mind and body by keeping the chakras balanced. There are seven chakras. The first is in the pelvic region and relates to the sexual organs and procreation. The second is in the belly button, controlling emotions. The third is in the solar plexus, ruling the stomach and digestive tract. The fourth is the heart chakra, which relates to love. The fifth, in the throat, relates to communication. The sixth is the third eye (the spot between the eyebrows) that rules higher consciousness. The seventh chakra is the crown chakra, which unites the person with the cosmic universe.

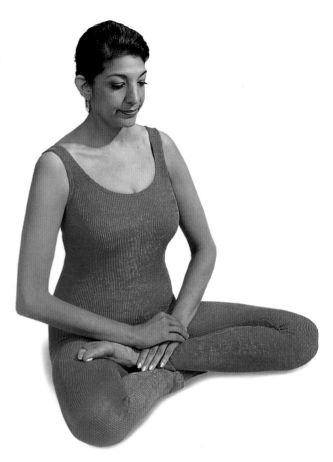

150

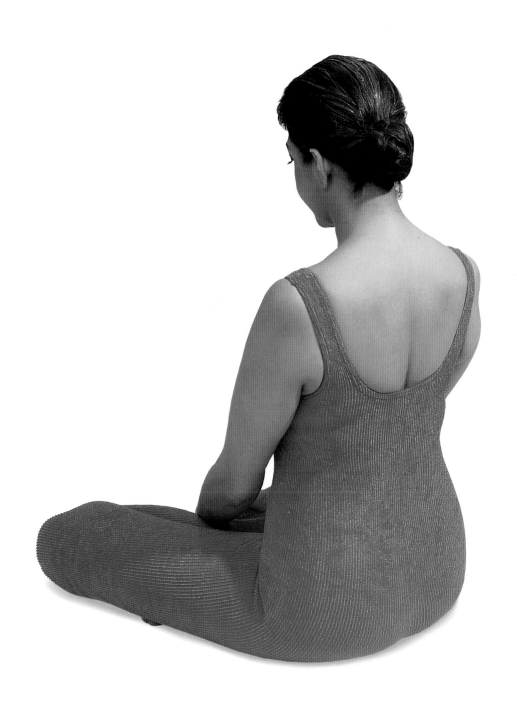

152

Meditation Poses

All meditation poses are sitting positions that vary only in how the legs are placed. Whether you are sitting cross-legged, in half-lotus or full lotus position, or with your heels together, your back must be erect from the base of your spine to your neck and be perpendicular to the floor. There should be no strain on the body. Keep your tongue still and your eyes closed. In meditation the brain is passive, but alert. If your organs are not functioning correctly the brain will send warning signals immediately. Meditation focuses the mind on one thought alone, and is useful to discipline and calm the mind. It is hard to sit still when your mind is wandering, but meditation teaches you how to shut yourself off from the world and find inner peace.

The first technique to learn is candle gazing. Place a candle in front of you so that the candle is in line with the point between your eyebrows. Now gaze at the candle and observe the flicker, the candle's size, and every aspect of it. After 30–60 seconds close your eyes. You will retain an optical image of the candle and the flicker of light in your mind. When the flicker starts to disappear, force the image to stay. This trains your mind to concentrate hard. At first it seems impossible to maintain the image but with continued practice it becomes easy. The next step is meditation. Focus your attention on the third eye and concentrate on one thought. Keep breathing deeply and notice your even breathing rhythm, while still focusing your mind on one thought.

Meditation poses

Top: Lotus
Left: Half-lotus
Right: Cross-legged
Bottom: Heels together

Remedial Yoga

Prana is the Sanskrit word for the energy that flows through the body. There are seven energy centers in the body and it is vital that energy flows freely through the system for good health. When people are stressed some centers become blocked, causing an imbalance. Yoga focuses on correct breathing techniques to increase the lung capacity and bring fresh oxygen to the vital organs. It is now possible to prove scientifically the effect of remedial yoga, and clinical trials have shown its beneficial results. There are four phases of stress disorders. The first is the psychic phase, in which irritability, energy loss, sleeplessness and anxiety attacks are manifested. If unchecked the person moves to the second, psychosomatic phase and experiences hypertension, tremors or palpitations. The next phase is the somatic phase, when illness develops in the vital organs. The fourth phase is the organic phase, when the affected organ is in full-fledged chronic inflammatory change. Medical attention is now required. Yoga can help prevent the first phase, relieve the symptoms in the second phase, develop a therapy programme in the third, and with modern medicine help the body return to its normal state in the fourth phase. Remedial yoga takes the stress disorder and applies a specific exercise that will alleviate the symptoms, or a series of exercises to help cure the ailment. Here I have prescribed the *asana* specific to some common ailments. There are some that respond particularly well, such as asthma, migraine and digestive disorders.

Head:
Headaches

When your head is pounding because of tension and other mental anxieties, dropping your head forward relieves the pressure in no time. The blood rushes to the brain and soothes the nervous system. Many people find this uncomfortable at first and may even feel dizzy and nauseous. In fact, it will probably feel as if the pain is increasing rather than decreasing. But do not panic, just give yourself time to get used to this sensation. Just breathe deeply throughout the exercise and the pain and panic will soon subside. Make sure you keep your weight evenly distributed between your heels and toes to maintain your balance. Keep your movements fluid and try not to pause between the positions.

Stand upright with your feet together in perfect posture (page 113). Inhale deeply and as you exhale drop your body forward. Bend your knees, relax your head and neck, shake out your arms and take your hands to the floor with your palms facing upward. Relax every muscle in your body. Hold for 30 seconds, breathing deeply. ▶ Slowly inhale and lift your body slowly upward, still keeping your head and arms forward. ▶ Now push your hips forward and drop your shoulders down. Then shift your weight to your heels, open out your chest and drop your head all the way back. Exhale, and breathe normally while you hold the position for 5 seconds. Lift up your head again and return to the start position. Repeat the whole exercise.

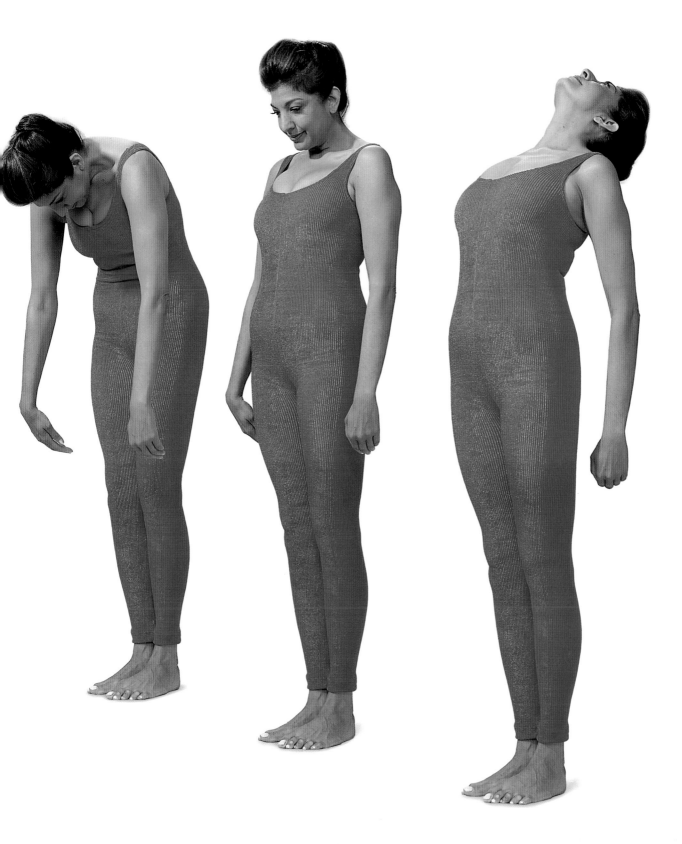

Head:
Mind

When people suffer from stress they can find it difficult to focus their mind for any length of time. Their thoughts are often confusing and conflicting. By doing balancing exercises you can help to focus your mind and improve your concentration. The concentration needed to stand on one leg can help you push distracting or negative thoughts from your mind. These exercises are quite challenging and at first you might think that you are incapable of balancing on one leg, but with perseverance you will soon reach your goal.

Stand up straight, feet together, in perfect posture (page 113). Breathe normally and draw your energies into yourself. Hold for 5 seconds. Place your right foot with your heel and toe in line with your left ankle. Place your palms together in front of your chest. Hold for 5 seconds. ▸ With your right hand lift your right leg and place it on your inner left lower leg, knee, or inner thigh according to your flexibility so that your knee is at right angles to the straight leg. Palms together, take your arms over your head and balance. Hold for 5–10 seconds and focus on an object in front of you to aid concentration. Repeat on the other side.

The one leg balance (see right) is more difficult. Stand upright with feet together. Take both hands to the floor to balance, clasp your right ankle anywhere on your leg and focus on one spot on the floor in front of you. ▸ Inhale, pull your tummy muscles in and lift your left leg up high without twisting your hips. Exhale and breathe normally. Repeat on the other side.

▶

158

Circulation:
Toxins

In yoga exercises, bending forward, sideways and backward allows every nerve, tissue and vein in the body to be replenished with fresh blood and oxygen. This purifies the system, releasing any harmful toxins that have become trapped. When you do this dynamic exercise you might think that you are simply perspiring, but you are actually eliminating toxins from your body. Some people may feel ill while exercising because drinking alcohol, using drugs, stress and bad eating habits all contribute to toxin buildup. If toxins are not removed, the immune system can break down, leading to serious illnesses.

Stand tall with feet 1–1.2m (3–4ft) apart. Inhale and bend your right knee, pushing your left foot firmly down to help you balance. Exhale. Inhale and take your hand down to the floor in front of your right foot. As you exhale, twist your body around so your shoulders are in line. ▸ Inhale, take your left arm up in the air with your palm facing back and continue to twist, looking over your left shoulder. Exhale and breathe normally. Straighten your arm and look upward toward the palm. ▸ Turn back toward your right leg, straighten your knee and clasp both elbows behind your back. Drop your forehead down to the knee. Breathe deeply and hold for 5–10 seconds. ▸ Inhale, and bring your body up so that your back is flat. Exhale, and breathe deeply for 5–10 seconds. ▸ Inhale, and bring your body up, then drop your head back to release your neck. Exhale, breathe normally and hold for 5 seconds. Repeat on the other side.

Circulation:
Joints

This simple swinging of the arms and body helps to increase circulation, particularly in your joints, hands and fingertips. If you suffer from stress-related rheumatism and arthritis, this exercise will ease the pain because the circular swing gradually loosens the joints. Yoga with its gentle approach will help shift the stiffness while relaxing the muscle groups through correct breathing. If your hip, knee or elbow joints are acutely inflamed, never try to force any movement. Just gently ease into the swing, breathing deeply to relax your mind and mobilize your entire body. Keep your feet still as you move the body around from one side to another.

Stand upright with your legs 1m (3ft) apart, your toes pointing forward and your arms at the side. Turn your body to the right and look over your right shoulder with your arm in line with the shoulder. ▶ Inhale and bring your right arm down. ▶ Exhale and begin to swing your arm across the front of your body in a circular motion and back up until it is in a diagonal line to your head, stretching to the left as you do so. While swinging, relax your knees and release your hips so that you have a wider swing. ▶ Inhale, then as you exhale keep stretching to the left, while twisting your spine. Breathe normally and hold for 10 seconds. Repeat the whole exercise on the other side. Practice the swing on both sides a few times until you feel that all your joints have been loosened.

Back:
Muscles

People who suffer from back pain are often worried that by exercising they will damage their backs even further. On the contrary, it is vital to strengthen back muscles in order to prevent strain and alleviate pain. Yoga provides a natural solution because of its emphasis on posture and correct alignment of the spine. While exercising you constantly build these muscles while noticing at all times the natural position of the spine. In order to stand or sit in perfect posture the muscles of the lower back must support the rest of the spine. Sciatica and slipped discs are a result of weakness in the back, and a strong, healthy back is necessary for total body health. This exercise strengthens the back while helping to increase flexibility. It also shapes the waist, hips and legs.

Start by standing tall with both feet together. Inhale, and drop your head down to your knees. Exhale and bend both knees. Inhale, simultaneously straightening your left leg directly behind you while lunging forward with the right. Point your left foot and keep your hips and torso facing to the front. Inhale, slowly twist your upper body to the left and look over your left shoulder. ▶ Now lift your left leg up and take hold of your toes. Exhale and balance for 5 seconds. Make sure that you are not balancing on your kneecap but on top of the knee to avoid any damage or strain. To release, turn to the front, place your fingertips on the floor and return to the start position. Repeat the exercise on the other side.

Back:
Tension

Twisting laterally alleviates back pain while strengthening the lower back. If you feel any discomfort you can modify these positions by bending both knees throughout. Once you have a back ailment any tension will aggravate it, so try to keep mentally relaxed at all times. All stress manifests itself in your body and backs are particularly prone to chronic conditions. Yoga in its holistic approach is one of the best ways to cope with back ailments, as relaxing and calming the mind and body eliminates emotions such as fear and anger which become trapped as tension in the muscle groups.

Start the exercise by lying flat on your back with your arms by your side. Take your arms out to the sides and put your palms face down on the floor, in line with your shoulders. Keeping your shoulders down, inhale and bend your right knee into your chest. Raise your head and, flexing your right thumb, clasp your big toe with your first two fingers. Make sure you keep your hips flat on the floor. ▶ Exhale and straighten the leg, still clasping your toe if you are able to. Hold for 5 seconds. Lower your head to the floor. ▶ Inhale again, and as you exhale take your leg to the right until it touches the floor at right angles to your body, still keeping your hips flat on the floor. Repeat the exercise on the other side.

Abdomen:
Stomach

Nervous tension in the stomach produces acidity, which can lead to gastric disorders such as flatulence, heartburn and irritable bowel syndrome. Doctors now agree that there is a direct link between the emotional balance of a person and their susceptibility to certain illnesses. People suffering from stomach aches are often emotionally upset. The stomach can seize up with muscle cramps and most people take medication to relieve their pain. Yoga relaxes the stomach cramps immediately because it teaches you to breathe through the pain in order to release it.

Lie flat on the floor. Inhale and bring both knees into your chest, lifting your head off the floor. Exhale and breathe normally for 10 seconds. ▸ Hold onto your right knee and place your left foot on the floor in front of your left hip. Inhale and bring your right knee closer in to your chest, pulling with your right hand on your knee and your left hand on your ankle. Exhale and hold for 5 seconds, breathing normally. ▸ Take both hands around the back of your right knee, inhale deeply and exhale, straightening the right leg. Breathe normally and hold for 10 seconds. ▸ Place your hands on your ankles, inhale and stretch your leg down toward your head. Exhale and bring your head up toward your leg. Breathe deeply and hold for 10 seconds, stretching until your forehead touches your knee. Release the leg down and repeat on the other side.

170

Abdomen:
Hormones

It is important to maintain a good hormonal balance during your life. During puberty, pregnancy and the menopause, hormone levels shift, causing emotional reactions and mood swings. Pre-menstrual syndrome is, in fact, more common today due to modern stress levels. Hormone replacements help, but can have side effects, whereas yoga naturally relieves the imbalance and stabilizes the hormonal levels. According to yogic texts, when the head is locked into the chest it stimulates the thyroid gland, balancing your metabolism. If you are more than three months pregnant, do not take your legs over your head as this alters the position of the uterus.

Lie flat on the floor. Bring your knees up but keep your feet on the floor with your arms at your sides.
▶ Inhale, bringing both knees into your chest, clasping your elbows under your knees. Exhale, lifting your head slightly off the floor. Breathe deeply; hold for 5 seconds. ▶ Breathe normally and straighten both legs, lifting your head up further. ▶ Take your hands to your waist for support and gently roll back, taking your legs over your head. Keep breathing deeply. Hold for 10–15 seconds. ▶ Inhale, tuck your toes under and lift your left leg up straight. Exhale, then breathe normally; hold for 10 seconds. Inhale, exhale and lower your left leg down. Inhale, and raise your right leg. Exhale, and breathe normally for 10 seconds. Release both knees into your chest and roll back down to the start position.

Respiration:
Stress

Ailments such as asthma and bronchitis are commonplace when stress factors affect the respiratory tract. Slowing your breathing down to an even pace while increasing the depth acts as a natural tranquilizer to the nervous system. Increasing your lung capacity also helps to relieve fatigue and hypertension. When people are fearful or panicky their heart races, their breathing becomes shallow and noisy, and they may pant. This exercise can help you to release tension and teaches you how to regulate your breathing pattern to reduce stress at a deeper level. You will then experience a sense of harmony and inner calm. Every time you repeat the exercise, breathe more deeply until you feel your lungs are filled to the brim.

Sit comfortably in a cross-legged position on the floor, or upright in a chair with both feet flat on the floor. It is important that your spine stays straight and your head is in line with your neck and back. Concentrate on your navel and inhale deeply, taking your arms up slowly around your body. Feel the breath moving to fill your lungs. ▶ Continuing to inhale, lift your arms up as you look upward. ▶ Clasp your fingertips together and continue to stretch upward. Exhale and drop your head back, releasing your hands in a burst of energy. Repeat this exercise 5–10 times.

Respiration:
Panic

The ability to relax and control your breathing pattern helps to reduce fear during a panic attack. The bronchial tubes allow fresh oxygen into the lungs while dispelling carbon dioxide. When an attack is imminent, the muscles in the walls of the tubes constrict the breath flow. When you are particularly active you can hear the change in your breath as you need more air to sustain your activity. On the other hand, when you are resting or sleeping, little air is required. If you feel an attack coming on, take your mind off it and calm your nervous system by breathing from the diaphragm. The muscles of the bronchial tubes will relax as you allow more breath to enter your lungs and your mental state will improve as you realize that you are in control of every reaction to the attack.

Stand tall in perfect posture (page 113). Stretch your arms high above your head, clasping your hands together. Keep your elbows straight and close to your ears. Force your shoulder blades down. Hold for 5 seconds, breathing normally. ▸ Inhale, and rise up on your toes. Breathe deeply; hold for 5 seconds, concentrating on balancing. ▸ Lift your heels higher as you bend your knees. ▸ Drop your heels down and stretch your hips backward as if reaching for a chair. The depth of your breathing will increase automatically. Keep your spine straight and your arms in line with your ears. Breathe deeply for 20 seconds. Repeat.

yoga for
better
sex

Yoga serves as a natural aphrodisiac and sexual conditioner that unites mind, body and soul. Though not everyone shares a spiritual dimension, everyone can experience the improvement that yoga brings to one's life, including its sexual dimension. In yoga, the union of mind and body is described through physical exercises, or *asanas*, to harmonize and balance the masculine and feminine energies; in Tantric yoga, harmony and balance are achieved through the sexual union between man and women. Not only does yoga promote a calm nervous system, it gives you the suppleness and flexibility that are required in lovemaking and also teaches you how to breathe correctly, bringing extra vitality and energy to the sexual act. The exercises in this chapter are designed to improve your sexual performance by increasing your stamina and your ability to stretch. The movements are graceful and fluid, like a dancer's, and are held for a length of time in order to allow the body's energy to alter. The yogic and sexual exercises both have the same goal; when they are intelligently and properly performed they will lead to longevity, alertness, radiant health and contentment.

Toning
Your Body

These exercises are designed to build muscle tone and
stamina and to increase your energy and vitality. When
you stretch and twist in all directions you tone your
internal organs and, combining that with correct
breathing, you send fresh oxygen to each nerve and cell,
rejuvenating the entire system. The sex center is located
in the lower spine and by strengthening the lower back
you will automatically improve your sexual performance.

There is much emphasis today on sexual accomplishment
and this is one area where money, status, fame, authority,
success, physical strength, and beauty are unable to play
a decisive role. While these factors may offer a wider
choice of partners, they cannot guarantee a good sexual
performance – and unfortunately the stresses and strains
which attend many of them are a contributory factor in
sexual disorders.

Confidence and sound mental health remain the greatest
assets in the successful consummation of the sex act.
Frigidity and fear of coitus in women and lack of an
erection or premature ejaculation in men are, in most
cases, psychological in origin. The regular practice of
yogic exercises will result in not only toning the neuro-
muscular structure of the sex organs of both men and
women but will rehabilitate the mind as well. Sexual
performance will improve when the mind, body, and soul
are integrated and the sexual partners are in total
harmony with their environment.

Balance

This balance combined with deep stretches will help focus your attention and steady your mind. Stretching is the best way to release tension in the muscle groups and this series of movements will increase suppleness and flexibility as well as building muscle tone.

Start the exercise in a wide second position.
▸ Turn your right foot to the right with your heel in line with the instep of your left foot. Take your arms behind your back with your palms facing together in a prayer position. This will automatically open the chest. Make sure your shoulders are down and your chin and head level. If you are unable to stretch your arms behind your upper back, hold onto your wrists and place them at your lower back. ▸ Inhale and drop your head back as far as possible. Relax your face and neck. ▸ Exhale and slowly lower your spine, stretching out from the waist, until your forehead touches your knee. Keep your left leg straight and pull up the muscle above your kneecap to help you maintain your balance. ▸ Keep your weight evenly distributed between both feet. Breathing normally, bend your right knee, keeping your head down to the knee. Make sure the back of your knee is directly above your heel. ▸ Release your arms from behind your back and place your right hand down to the floor in line with your shoulder to steady your balance. Fix one point on the floor and concentrate your gaze. Take your left hand to your waist. ▸ Inhale, straighten your right leg and at the same time lift your left leg up so your spine is in a straight line. Flex your left foot. Exhale and hold this position for 10 seconds. To release, return to position 5 and slowly return to the starting position with arms at your sides. Repeat the entire exercise on the other side.

Pelvic Stretch

The pelvic stretch tones the sex organs and the kidneys, aids digestion and rejuvenates the spine. After childbirth or with advancing age, many women suffer from incontinence, a lack of tightness in the vaginal wall and a loss of sensation during sexual intercourse. Learning how to isolate and contract the pelvic muscle will greatly improve these conditions.

Kneel down on the floor, spreading your feet as far apart as you can while keeping your knees together. Place your hands behind you and sit erect. Breathe deeply and evenly. ▸ Keeping your knees together, slowly lower yourself, leaning on your elbows. You will feel a stretch in the feet, ankles, knees, thighs, abdomen, and ribs. If you feel comfortable, stretch further down to the floor, taking your arms over your head, holding your elbows. As you breathe deeply and especially during the exhalation you will feel a deep stretching sensation throughout your whole body. This intense stretch sends a fresh blood supply to the entire system and the effect is soothing, tranquil, and deeply relaxing. ▸ To release yourself from this position return to position 2, then 1. Now relax down to the floor with your arms to the side, palms facing down. Raise your knees with your feet in line with your hips. ▸ Inhale, hold onto your ankles, and raise your pelvis as high as possible. Exhale, breathe normally, tighten your stomach and buttock muscles and contract the muscles in the sex centers. Hold for 10 seconds and slowly lower to the floor by pushing down each vertebra of the spine, starting from the neck. Repeat the entire exercise, then move on to the exercises on pages 184–5.

Lying on the floor, bring your knees into your chest. Cross your ankles and hold onto your feet.
▸ Inhale, and take your knees down to the floor. Exhale, and hold for 5 seconds, breathing normally.
▸ Inhale, and push up your chest until the top of your head is on the floor. In classic yoga, this pose is called the Fish; it helps corrects certain defects of the spine and sends fresh oxygen and blood supply to the brain, which soothes the nerves. Exhale, breathe normally and lower your back to the floor to return to the previous position. Repeat the exercise. ▸ Now release the legs and lie flat on the floor. Inhale, point both feet and raise the left leg up off the floor toward your head, then raise your upper body off the floor toward the leg. Lift your right leg 30cm (1ft) off the floor. Exhale, breathe normally and hold for 5 seconds. Slowly lower your back down to the floor and lift both legs in a right angle to the body. Breathe deeply and hold for 10 seconds. Inhale, lift your body up and hold onto your right ankle, stretching your head to your right knee. Exhale and lower your left leg down to 30cm (1ft) from the floor. Point both feet, breathe deeply and hold for 5 seconds. Raise your left leg until both legs are in a 90° angle to the floor. Bend both knees into the chest. Inhale, and as you exhale slowly lower the legs down to the floor. Relax for 10 seconds.

pelvic stretch

Prelude

There is deep communication between partners who have an understanding of the philosophy of yoga, as yoga-controlled relationships achieve a high quality of cultural and spiritual life. Deep satisfaction steadies and tranquilizes the mind, and feelings of love and consideration can develop more easily; Tantric sex will accelerate these emotions and will raise the conscious level of both partners.

The techniques of Tantra were originally used by the sages and mystics to reach Nirvana, or union with God. The aim was to take the basic energy or sex energy from the base chakra and transform it into spiritual energy. Ritualistic practices were learned to raise the conscious level to a higher plane. One of the secrets of Tantra was to know how to arouse different parts of the body and play the partner's body like an instrument to create notes and sensations. So, using the arts of Tantra, two people aimed to work together to raise the sound of their bodies and their vibrations.

Even today, Tantric practices can be used by ordinary people who wish to experience mystical or ecstatic sex. One of the techniques in reaching this goal is total abstinence from sex. The couple sit directly across from one another and keep their eyes fixed on each other. As they breathe deeply their sexual vibrations unite and with meditation they begin to raise together their energy through all chakras to the crown to connect with the cosmic vibration. This gives a feeling of divine bliss and harmony with the universe.

Double Leg Pull

The Leg Pull requires a great deal of practice to perfect as it combines increased flexibility and stamina with concentration. It is a challenging exercise and you should not be surprised if you and your partner fall down; it is always very important when you are practicing yoga to maintain your sense of humor! It is an enjoyable and exhilarating feeling to master a particularly difficult exercise and it is great fun to practice with your partner. The Leg Pull also promotes positive thinking and this attitude helps to boost the confidence and self-esteem that are necessary for a good relationship.

Begin the exercise with both partners standing together in perfect posture (page 113). ▸ Place your left hand on your waist, inhale and lift your right foot up to the inner thigh of your left leg. Exhale and hold for 5 seconds. ▸ Inhale and take your first two fingers around your toe. Exhale and hold the position for 5 seconds, standing as tall as you can. ▸ Inhale and as you exhale extend the leg outward. Keep the hips in line and try not to cave in the chest; the standing leg must remain straight. If you cannot extend the raised leg fully, keep it bent. With increased flexibility and practice you will eventually be able to hold the position for at least 7 seconds. Release, bend the right leg in a 90° angle and return to perfect posture. Repeat on the other side.

Double Head to Knee

This pose lengthens and tones the entire spine and relaxes the brain. It opens the hips and strengthens the leg muscles. All forward bends help to release toxins that are trapped in the system and this forward action stimulates the kidneys, liver and pancreas. When you first begin this exercise you might feel disappointed that you are unable to bend very far, but with continued practice and correct breathing you will be surprised at how flexible your spine becomes. Never push or jerk your body to increase the stretch as this might cause strain to your muscles; as you increase the depth of your breathing you will automatically relax and this will loosen tight muscles in the legs and lower back and you will stretch even further. Keep your feet firmly placed on the floor and distribute your weight evenly between your heels and toes. As you stretch forward, think of moving your spine out from your tail bone. This will help to flatten and lengthen the spine.

Stand tall back-to-back with your partner and check to make sure you are in perfect posture (page 113). Breathe normally and hold hands to give each other support. ▶ Inhale, keeping your spine as flat as possible, then exhale and bend forward halfway. Hold for 5 seconds while you breathe normally. ▶ Take a deep breath and as you exhale drop your head down to your knees. Continue to breathe deeply and hold this position for 30 seconds. To release, inhale slowly, bend the knees, curl the spine and gently unroll it until you have reached the first position. Repeat the entire exercise once.

The Locust

A good sexual performance demands a very strong back, especially in the ardent poses of the Kama Sutra. The Locust not only helps to alleviate back pain but strengthens the back and legs so you are able to build endurance and stamina. It also helps to improve your posture by strengthening the lower back so you are able to sit and stand for a length of time. It is important to learn to isolate certain muscle groups and in this exercise, even though every muscle is working, there is an emphasis on the stomach, legs and buttocks. Do not worry if you cannot lift your legs very high behind you – it is more important that your shoulder blades and hipbones remain on the floor to ensure that your spine is in correct alignment. As you practice this pose you will be able to lift your leg higher. Think of stretching your leg out from the hipbone and make sure you do not rock from side to side.

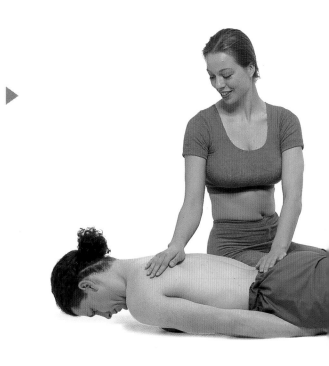

Begin the exercise by lying face down on the floor, your hands under your hipbones. Your partner should watch to see that your spine is perfectly straight. ▸ Inhale, and raise your right leg off the floor. Exhale, breathe normally and hold for 5 seconds. Exhale and slowly lower the leg down to the floor. Inhale, raise the left leg and hold for 5 seconds. Exhale and slowly lower the left leg. Repeat. ▸ Ask your partner to make sure both hips are down to the floor, then inhale deeply and raise both legs. Hold for 5–10 seconds. Exhale and slowly lower both legs. This is quite a strenuous exercise and your heartbeat should be racing. Relax and turn your head to one side until your pulse is normal. Repeat the entire exercise.

Double Sitting Twist

All twists are excellent for increasing flexibility of the spine and eliminating toxins from the system. They are very effective in relieving backaches and headaches as well as stiffness in the neck and shoulders. As the upper body turns, the kidneys and abdominal organs are activated, aiding digestion and removing sluggishness. The beauty of twists is that there is no final position because as you become more supple your twist increases. There are many variations to the classic twist, but all alleviate back pain and inflexibility of the lower back. It is a great pleasure to hear the clicks in the spine when you release tension. You cannot be a good sex partner if you are full of anxieties and this twist eliminates the stresses and strains that build up in the body. The most important thing is your determination to rid yourself of tension. Once you have won the first battle with your mind, your body will surely follow.

Sit up as tall as possible with your legs extended in front of you, side-to-side but facing slightly away from each other. ▸ Both of you then bend the outermost leg to create a 90° angle with your knee and hip. ▸ Take the outermost arm across in front of the innermost knee and gently twist the spine. ▸ Lift the innermost leg up and place the foot in front of the outermost knee. Continue to stretch as far as possible. Breathe as deeply as you can and relax into the stretch. Hold for up to 60 seconds. Change sides and repeat.

Leg Stretch

In lovemaking it is so important to trust your partner even if the poses are difficult. There is a healthy give and take in this pose which will give you both a sense of balancing and harmonizing each other's energy in preparation for the sexual poses that follow. This stretch increases the flexibility and suppleness of the spine and strengthens the legs and back. It also stretches and tones the internal organs. Because you are putting your full weight onto each other you are helping your partner stretch forward without strain while you are working on stretching your entire body backward and opening the chest. In yoga, the importance of opening the chest is to steady the emotional center or heart chakra that lies just below the physical heart. The final position opens this center and stabilizes emotional disturbances. The mind becomes still as if you were in a meditative pose.

Sit tall back-to-back with your legs outstretched, pointing your toes in front of you. ▸ Bring your knees up while keeping your feet flat on the floor. Lean back onto your partner's upper back so he or she will automatically move forward. Push your feet down to the floor, raise your hips and lean back even further. ▸ Stretch your legs out fully and place your entire weight onto your partner's spine, arching your back. Take your arms over your head to increase the stretch. This movement will help your partner stretch forward, placing the forehead down to the knees. If your partner finds this uncomfortable, modify the pose by taking some of the weight yourself. Change positions with your partner and repeat the entire exercise.

Half Lotus Side Stretch

This pose is an excellent exercise for toning your entire body and calming your central nervous system. In yoga exercises you are continually moving your whole body in every direction: forward, backward, sideways. This twisting and turning of the spine strengthens the nerves and helps build the immune system. A healthy sex life is based on good health generally and when you feel well you will perform better. As you stretch to the side and front in this exercise, try not to collapse your spine. Always stretch from the tail bone and elongate each muscle to eliminate the fat around each muscle group. The result will be a lean, muscular body that is tight and firm.

Begin these stretches by sitting back-to-back as you did in the Leg Stretch (pages 196–7). Breathe normally. Place your right foot on the left thigh or left foot on the right thigh in the Half Lotus and twist your spine to look at your partner. Slide your bent leg down to the floor, keeping your knee in line with your hip. ▶ Inhale and stretch over the outstretched leg. Take your upper arm over your head close to your ear and lower your other arm to the floor. Exhale and take your fingertips to clasp your feet. Breathe normally and hold the position for 10 seconds. ▶ Now face your extended knee. Inhale, and stretch forward so your forehead touches your knee. Exhale and clasp your hands together behind your feet. Breathe deeply and evenly and hold this position for 10 seconds or for as long as you feel comfortable. Change sides and repeat the entire sequence.

Back Arch

This Back Arch immediately restores vitality and energy to the system and relaxes the brain. It also allows you and your partner to help each other improve your suppleness. When your back is arched and your head dropped to the floor behind you, the blood rushes to your brain, revitalizing and replenishing your brain cells. It is impossible to be a good lover when your sex drive is low or there is a lack of enthusiasm, and this exercise is an excellent tonic to refresh your mind when you are feeling lethargic and tired. It also allows you to move intimately with your partner which will set the mood for lovemaking. When you are helping each other to stretch, be aware of each other's capabilities – in many cases the flexibility of the couple may not be equal. Never force or push your partner; remember that yoga is non-competitive and everyone should always work at their own pace. With continued practice and patience you will see how fast you progress.

Begin by sitting facing each other and hold one another in a gentle, loving manner. Take your legs over each other's thighs and bring both feet together. ▶ With your partner holding your lower back for support, inhale, arch your back and lift up as high as possible to rest on the top of your head. Exhale and breathe normally. This improves circulation to the face and neck and you will feel the blood flow into the brain. Hold for 5–10 seconds. ▶ Inhale, release the neck and have your partner help you back up. Exhale and relax your spine forward as your partner arches the spine and relaxes backward. Repeat the exercise 5 times with a back-and-forth motion.

Heart Chakra

It is very important in lovemaking to be in tune mentally and emotionally with your partner. Tantric sex unites your energy centers and it is vital that these centers remain unblocked. There are seven chakras in the body and the heart chakra lies in the center of the chest. It is the energy center that rules compassion and unconditional love, and blocked energy here leads to psychological and emotional disturbances. This exercise balances all seven centers from the base or pelvic region, through the navel into the solar plexus, through the heart into the throat, and through the third eye (between the eyebrows) into the top of the head or crown to unite with the cosmic or universal energy. This technique is used as a ritual in Tantra to arouse sexual passion and heighten sexual pleasure.

Begin by sitting cross-legged, facing each other, with enough distance between you to prevent you from touching each other. ▶ Sit up as tall as possible and clasp your hands together, palms facing outwards. ▶ Concentrating on your base chakra, inhale deeply and slowly raise your arms, moving through each chakra until you raise your arms high over your head. Keep the breath even and continuous as you slowly fill your lungs with air. Exhale and slowly bring the arms back down to position 1. Try to match the exact pace of your partner while performing the exercise. Repeat up to 10 times.

Love Poses

Sexual positions, or Kama *asanas*, bring variety and
excitement to the sex act. In the *Kama Sutra*, the great
sage Vatsyayana describes the ways to achieve
pleasure through a systematic and scientific approach
to the anatomy of the body and the reactions of the
mind. While the sex urge is a natural and powerful
phenomenon, it can be disciplined by the gift of yoga.
Within these sexual poses it is important to prolong the
sex act and to increase pleasure by observing and
understanding it. If you are already acquainted with
the yoga positions you should not find the *Kama Sutra*
poses illustrated here difficult, and the benefits you
gain will be enhanced when you achieve the fulfilment
of Kama or sexual bliss. To condemn knowledge of sex
as a sin, and to glorify ignorance as bliss, merely
promotes misery, incompetence, fear and damage to
the psyche. No man should think of sexual intercourse
as the supreme test of his manliness, nor should a
woman regard it as her badge of femininity. If you
feel an act of sex to be a test or competition, the
spontaneity and the naturalness of the situation will be
destroyed. Embrace it as a wonderful and integral part
of a healthy and rounded life and enjoy the pleasure
that is a fundamental right for each human being.

Splits Love Pose

This beautiful love pose is a perfect blend of a dancer's grace and poise combined with the flexibility of the hips and groin. To achieve this pose it is important for the woman to practice the Half Lotus Side Stretch (page 198–9) and Double Sitting Twist (pages 194–5) to release stiffness and help open up the hip area.

The man kneels down on the floor with his knees close together and his hips touching his heels, his feet flat down behind him. The woman half kneels down close to him on his left side so their bodies are touching and their arms caressing one another, she with her right arm around his right shoulder and her left arm on his right forearm and he with his left hand on her back and his right hand on her waist. ▸ She lunges her right leg over his thighs, creating a right angle to the floor, making sure that her lunge is deep enough so her knee does not extend over her foot. She balances on her left knee and her left hand moves to her waist, covering his hand. ▸ From this position she slides her right leg in a perfectly straight line and extends her left leg behind her until her weight is fully on his body. She points both her feet and balances between her right heel and left knee. She gently lifts her spine up toward her partner so her back is leaning on his chest, reaches her arms behind her and takes her right arm around the man's head in order to twist her body toward him so she can still gaze lovingly into his eyes.

The Swan Love Pose

In order to achieve this love pose it is important for the woman to practice the Standing Bow (pages 72–3) and the Locust (pages 192–3) in order to improve the strength and flexibility of her lower back and the Double Sitting Twist (pages 194–5) to help rotate her spine easily. Some people might find the final position too difficult to achieve and so finish with position 2 instead.

The couple begin the pose sitting down on the floor or a divan holding each other in a loving manner. The woman sits in front of the man, leaning on her left buttock with both legs tucked under so her knees and feet are together. She leans on the man and turns her back toward him so her right cheek caresses the left side of his face. He sits upright with his left leg up in a 90° angle to the floor in line with his left hip, and his right leg folded directly in front of him. He holds the woman firmly and she gently holds his hands. ▶ She lifts herself up on both knees and slides her body on to his right thigh. She extends her right leg behind her as far as possible while balancing her weight between her left leg and her partner's upper thigh.. He drops his right hand to the floor and straightens his elbow in order to support her weight. She turns her back so she can face him and puts her right hand behind his head. ▶ She reaches behind his back and lifts her right foot up and arches her spine. She holds on to her foot and twists her body closer to his body. He takes his left hand to his left leg and kisses her gently on the mouth.

Half-Standing Love Pose

People who are relatively fit can achieve this pose without too much difficulty. Because of its simplicity it allows the intimacy of the couple to flourish as well as heightening sexual desire. The couple can concentrate fully on their sexual pleasure and balance their weight equally between them.

The couple begin by standing facing each other. The man drops to his left knee and keeps the right knee up with his foot firmly placed on the floor in a right angle to the floor. The woman lifts her left leg up and places her left foot on his right hipbone with her toes facing outward and her heel next to his groin. Her standing leg remains straight. She takes her right arm around his left shoulder and he takes his right hand to her left buttock. She gazes down at him and holds his right hand gently. ▸ She steps over his right thigh with her left leg and lowers herself down to his pelvis so her weight is resting on his body. Her left foot is firmly placed on the floor and her right leg is bent in order to distribute her weight evenly and allow movement between them. He grips her tightly around her waist and draws her closely toward him. She puts her left hand on his right knee for support and pulls herself closer to him. ▸ She drops down to her right knee and curves her left leg around his waist so their bodies are directly touching. She points her toes and he takes hold of her foot with his left hand. He draws her body even closer as they gaze directly into each other's eyes.

Leg Hook Love Pose

This erotic love pose unites the couple with equal passion and is relatively simple to perform. Both partners need to have a similar amount of strength in their arms and legs as well as in their pelvic and abdominal muscles. The Pelvic Stretch (pages 182–3) is a good exercise to help strengthen these muscle groups and the Dog Pose (pages 36–7) is particularly useful for building stamina and straightening the arms and legs.

To begin this pose the man sits on the floor with his knees facing outward and the soles of his feet together. The woman sits on top of the man with her feet also placed soles together. Their arms are gently wrapped around each other, his at her lower back and hers around the middle of his back. ▸ The woman leans back and places both her hands to the floor with her fingers pointing to the man. She straightens her arms in order to support her weight, lifts both legs up off the floor and places them on either side of her partner's head to rest on his shoulders. Both legs are exactly parallel and she is slightly off the ground, balancing on her hands. He moves his hands to her upper back to prepare to lift her and gazes directly into her eyes. ▸ Pushing down on her palms, she extends her elbows and lifts her body off the floor. When she is perfectly steady and balanced the man lifts his legs over her shoulders around her neck and places his hands behind him in order to free his hips and give himself extra support. The heads of the man and woman are at the same level to allow freedom of movement.

Half Plough Love Pose

This pose combines the classic Shoulder Stand (pages 76–7) for the woman and the Warrior pose (page 42) for the man. The pose is dramatic in feeling and looks as if the man is dominating the woman. In reality it is a beautiful exchange of energy that is both erotic and sensuous.

The woman begins by lying flat on the floor, legs together and arms at her sides. She bends her knees to her chest, places her hands in the small of the back to support her spine and rolls back into an inverted position so her knees are on the top of her forehead. (If the abdominal muscles are weak she can place her hands on the floor to push herself back and then replace the hands on her lower back.) She lifts both legs up so her spine is as straight as possible, points her feet and locks her chin into her chest. The man stands close and pushes his weight under her hips to help straighten her spine even further. He holds her upper thigh with his right hand and both ankles with his left hand. ▸ The woman lowers her right leg to the floor directly behind her head, pointing her foot to extend her leg in a straight line. The man checks her position to make sure that she is in a 90° angle to the floor. ▸ When he is confident that her position is correct he lunges his left leg over her groin in front of her right leg and lowers himself. His left hand moves down to her inner thigh and his right hand holds on to her left ankle. He is now at a perfect angle to look into her eyes.

214

Side Love Pose

The beauty of this pose lies in its simplicity and truth. As the pose requires little movement it is a perfect opportunity for the couple to connect with each other's energy flow. In the Heart Chakra pose (pages 202–3) the energy contact flows through the chakras to unite at the level of the crown. Meditate on this thought and feel as if you are uniting sexually to connect with the universal cosmic flow of energy. Keep the eye contact constant and you will have a feeling of floating into divine bliss.

The man begins this pose by sitting comfortably on the floor, his legs outstretched in front of him and his spine erect. The woman sits sideways on the left side of his lap so her legs and feet are together alongside his right hip. The man takes his arms lovingly around her hips and the woman places her arms around his shoulders. They gaze deeply into each other's eyes. ▸ The woman leans back and places her left hand on the floor to support her weight. She bends her left leg and wraps it tightly around the man's waist. She lifts her right leg and points her foot over his left shoulder so her leg is in a straight line. The man takes his right palm to the floor to support the change in the woman's movement. They are still looking directly at each other. ▸ With his right arm, the man grasps the middle of the woman's back to draw her closer. She places her left foot on the floor to support her weight and give herself freedom to move. She takes her right arm around his shoulder so she can grip on to his body, and points her toe harder to straighten her knee. They continue to gaze lovingly at one another.

stay
youthful
with
yoga

The quest for eternal youth is universal. Even the earliest records of human civilizations provide evidence of elixirs and potions used to preserve youth and beauty, while numerous scientists today are engaged in a search for new techniques with which to hold the ageing process at bay. Millions of pounds are spent by the public each year on anti-ageing creams and body treatments and some people resort to cosmetic surgery to restore the appearance of youth. There is a proverb in yoga philosophy that says that the day you begin your yoga practice the age clock stops. Yoga can counteract the effects of time by regulating your metabolism, balancing your hormonal levels and raising your energy reserves, focusing your mind and keeping your spine supple. As the spine becomes more flexible, energy flows more freely throughout the system, increasing vitality, while correct breathing rejuvenates the entire body and mind. Yoga is more than mere exercise. It can boost the immune system and help to stop ill health occurring in all age groups. If ailments do occur, yoga can help to alleviate the symptoms and in some cases can even eliminate the condition.

Daily Exercises

This section of the book offers six exercise routines with different objectives, each taking about 10 minutes to do. Day One improves the circulation to prevent stiffness in the joints; Day Two tones the parts of the body that show the first signs of ageing; Day Three strengthens the lower back to alleviate back pain; Day Four opens the chest area to unblock trapped energy in the spine; Day Five energizes the entire system; and finally Day Six teaches correct breathing to rejuvenate the system.

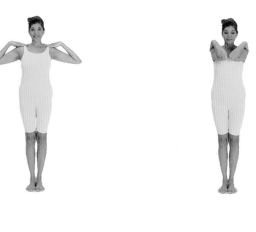

Day One:
Circulation

People who have good circulation feel robust, happy and healthy, while those with poor circulation may feel constantly depleted of energy and this affects their mental attitude. Fear of immobility and of growing old plagues even the happiest of people from time to time and so it is important to keep the body active and circulation flowing evenly. Poor circulation is a common complaint which can lead to various illnesses, so in this section I have designed a series of movements to boost your energy levels, raise your spirits and reoxygenate your entire system. You will notice that you are moving and twisting in every direction, which will stimulate all the internal organs and nerves, and combining this with deep breathing to release tension in the body.

Stand with your feet together in perfect posture (page 113). Take your hands onto your shoulders, keeping the elbows up in a straight line to each other. ▸ Inhale and bring your elbows in toward each other. Exhale, and push the elbows back as far as possible to open the chest. ▸ Looking upward, clasp your hands behind your head, lifting your elbows up as high as possible without lifting the shoulders. ▸ Inhale and bring your elbows toward each other, keeping your arms as close to the head as possible. ▸ Exhale and open your elbows wide, keeping your elbows in line and the shoulders down. ▸

223

Place your feet 1–1.2 m (3–4 ft) apart, toes pointing forward. Standing tall with your spine erect, place your right hand on your waist and take your left arm to the side in an exact line to the shoulder. Turn your palm upward and gaze toward your hand. ▸ Inhale and in a fluid movement take your arm in a circular movement over your head, stretching as far as possible to the right side. Inhale and exhale and hold for 10 seconds. Release the body, stand tall, place your left hand to your waist and repeat to the other side. Keep your breathing deep and even as you stretch further to the left. ▸ Take the left hand down to the right ankle and twist, looking over the right shoulder. Repeat on the other side. ▸ Return to standing position. Cross your arms in front of your chest with your palms facing toward you. ▸ Inhale, and with a graceful movement bring your arms down in line with the hips and up in a straight line to your shoulders. ▸ Push your shoulders down and extend your arms as much as possible. Make sure your fingertips are together and your palms facing down. Exhale, breathe normally and hold for 5 seconds. ▸

224

225

Bend your left elbow, inhale and as you exhale reach down to your right ankle. ▶ Place your left hand on your right ankle and twist, looking over your right shoulder. If you are unable to reach the ankle, place your left hand anywhere on your right leg. Inhale and exhale deeply as you increase the twist. Hold for 7 seconds. ▶ Return to standing position with arms outstretched to the side then take your right hand to your left ankle and repeat the twist on the other side.

▶ Release the twist and take both arms down in front of you, keeping your hands parallel in line with your shoulders.

▶ Inhale and slowly reach forward from the tail bone, bringing your arms upward over your head, palms facing each other. Exhale, breathe normally and hold for 3 seconds. ▶ Keeping the arms in the exact position, turn your right foot to the right and left foot slightly inward. Make sure your right heel is in a direct line to the instep of your left foot. Turn your body all the way to the right so both hips are facing to the right. ▶

227

Bring your palms together in prayer position and cross your thumbs. Bend your right knee, making sure it does not overextend the right foot. ▸ Inhale, straighten your right leg and point your left foot as much as possible. This will help your left leg to remain straight. ▸ Exhale and lift your left leg up behind you, balancing on your right leg. Keep your arms in line with your head, close to your ears. Breathing deeply, continue to stretch in both directions so your spine is in a straight line with your arms and foot. Hold the position for 10 seconds and deepen the breath as the pose increases in intensity. ▸ To release, bend your right knee and take your left foot back to starting position. Straighten your right leg and

place both hands behind your lower back in prayer position, fingers pointing upward. Inhale and take your head back, pushing your chest and hips forward. ▸ Exhale and, leading with the chin, stretch forward from the tail bone so your spine remains in a straight line. Breathe normally and hold for 5 seconds. ▸ Inhale, drop your head forward and stretch down toward your right knee. Exhale, breathe deeply and hold for 5 seconds. Inhale, release the spine and continue to stretch forward, keeping your spine straight. As you return to the starting position, push your hips forward and drop your head backward. Exhale, breathe normally and straighten your spine. Repeat the entire exercise on the other side.

229

Day Two:
Toning

As we age our muscles begin to sag and it is vital to tone and strengthen them. Stretching is the best way to achieve top-to-toe fitness and yoga stretches the muscles lengthways, reducing the fat around each muscle and producing a long, lean, streamlined body. It also increases the flexibility and suppleness of the spine so that your movements are more fluid and graceful. A further benefit is that deep stretching stimulates lymphatic drainage which helps to eliminate cellulite, a common problem for women of all ages. The exercises in this section tone the areas of the body that show the signs of ageing first – legs, thighs, buttocks and tummy. The twisting movements help eliminate toxins from the system and the deep stretching movements increase circulation.

When toning the body it is very important to concentrate on the muscle groups you wish to firm. When you stand in perfect posture make sure every muscle in the body is working by lifting each muscle upward, especially the muscle above the kneecap. Tighten your tummy muscles and tuck your tail bone under while you imagine a string pulling you upward from the top of your head. Place your feet 30 cm (1 ft) apart, directly in line with your hips. Cross your arms in front of your chest, holding on to your elbows. ▶ Focus your attention on a spot in front of you. Rise up on your toes, lifting your heels up as high as possible. ▶ Now, keeping your spine in a straight line, bend your knees, lifting your heels up in a right angle to the floor. Hold the position, breathing deeply and evenly, for at least 10 seconds. You will find this position very challenging because you are combining balance with deep breathing. ▶ Now take the legs in a wide second position with your feet 1–1.2 m (3–4 ft) apart. Take your arms out to the side, in line with your shoulders. ▶ Turn your right foot to the right, making sure it is in an exact line to the instep of your left foot. Look over your right hand while keeping your spine upright. ▶

232

Leading from the tail bone, stretch out to the right as far as possible. ▶ Take your right hand down to your ankle and take your left arm upward in a straight line. Make sure your fingertips are together and your palm is facing forward. Breathe deeply and normally as you hold for 7–10 seconds. ▶ Take your left arm over your head close to your ear in a straight line to the spine. Keep looking upward as you inhale and exhale deeply for 10 seconds. ▶ Bend your right knee in an exact right angle so the back of the knee is in line to the right heel. Take your right palm to your instep and as you stretch diagonally take your left arm in an exact line to your left leg. Hold the pose for 10 seconds. ▶ Now take your right arm to join your left arm in a parallel line and hold the position while your breath deepens. Hold for 5 seconds. ▶ Clasp your hands together as you increase the stretch. Hold the position and breathe as deeply as possible for at least 10 seconds. ▶

Lift your spine in a straight line as you clasp your hands over your head. Deepen the stretch as you lift your spine upward to be as tall as possible. Inhale and straighten your knee and turn your body forward. Release your arms and take them to your sides. ▸ Lie back on the floor and relax your whole body, keeping your arms next to your body on either side. Inhale and lift your left leg upward in an exact 90° angle to the floor. Clasp your hands together behind your knee and point your toes upward. Hold for 5 seconds. ▸ Bend your right knee and bring your heel in as close to your right buttock as possible. ▸ Inhale and stretch your head to your left knee, keeping your leg in a straight line. Hold for 7 seconds, breathing deeply and evenly. Slowly lower your spine and then release your left leg down to the floor. Relax your right leg

so both legs are down to the floor. Repeat the exercise on the other side. Inhale and exhale as you relax down. ▸ Bring both knees up, keeping your arms to your sides. ▸ Concentrate on your hips and tighten your buttock muscles as you lift your hips as high as possible. Breathing deeply, keep lifting the buttock muscles upward. Hold your ankles if you are able to reach them – if not, hold anywhere along the leg that is comfortable. Draw your chin into your chest as you continue to lift your hips upward. You are now in a perfect circular pose. To release, isolate the spine by pushing each vertebra down from the top of the spine so the tail bone is last to return to the floor. ▸

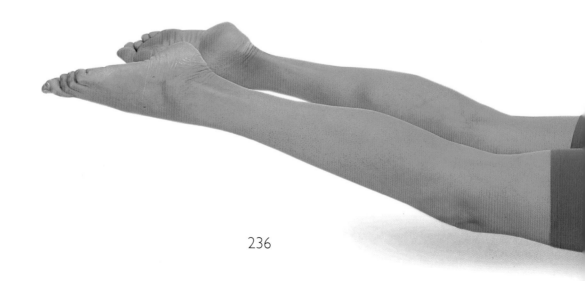

236

Release your hands from your ankles and relax your legs down to the floor. Inhale and exhale deeply for 5 seconds. ▸ Bring your legs together and point your toes down. Take your arms to your sides, palms on the floor. Inhale, push down on your elbows and raise your chest as high as possible so you are able to balance on the top of your head. Exhale, breathe normally and hold for 5–7 seconds. This is called the Fish pose and is an excellent stretch for the neck and chin. ▸ Turn over onto your stomach and place your chin on the floor. Place your hands in fists at your sides.

▸ Inhale, point your left foot to help straighten your knee and raise your left leg off the floor, keeping both hipbones down. Exhale, breathe normally and hold for 5–7 seconds. On an exhalation, slowly lower your leg. Repeat on the other side. ▸ Take your arms out to the side and rest on your elbows, fingers pointing inward. ▸ Inhale and simultaneously lift both legs and your chest off the floor, taking your arms behind you. Exhale, breathe deeply and hold for at least 10 seconds. This is an excellent exercise for toning and lifting the buttock muscles. Repeat and hold for 12–15 seconds.

Day Three:
Strengthening the Back

People who suffer from chronic back pain often believe that they should refrain from doing any exercise. In fact, it is vital to strengthen the muscles in the back to alleviate pain and prevent further back injuries. The exercises in this section are designed to eliminate the fear of moving the spine forward and backward. They will remove any muscular tension trapped in the back, relieve stiffness in the neck and shoulders and strengthen the muscles in the lower back to enable you to sit and stand in perfect posture. Pay special attention to all the muscles in the spine and perform slow, deliberate movements, taking deep and even breaths throughout. A dull pain in the spine merely indicates that your muscles are working, but if you feel any sharp pain stop the exercises immediately.

Stand with your feet together in perfect posture, arms to the side. Inhale and lift your arms up in front of you in line with your shoulders. Make sure your elbows are straight and your palms are facing down. Exhale, breathe normally and hold for 3 seconds. ▸ Concentrate on the area of the lower back and reach forward from the tail bone, keeping your spine straight and tightening your tummy muscles as you stretch down. ▸ Using your natural body weight combined with deep inhalations and exhalations to loosen the spine, stretch right down so your hands reach the floor. Do not force or jerk your body down. You will be surprised how supple your spine will soon

238

become. ► Bend your knees, drop your head forward and place your palms either side of your feet. ► Inhale, tighten your tummy muscles, hold on to your ankles and gently draw your forehead down to your knees. Exhale, breathe deeply and hold for 5–7 seconds. ►

Release your hands and begin to uncurl your spine slowly, keeping your knees straight. ▸ Pull your tummy muscles up, tighten your buttock muscles, drop your shoulders and lift your head up. ▸ When you are standing tall, take both arms behind your lower back, holding firmly on to your elbows. ▸ Inhale and push your hips forward as much as possible. Keep your knees straight, open your chest and drop your head back. Exhale, breathe normally and relax your neck and jaw. Hold for 5–7 seconds. Slowly release by returning to standing position and relax forward to counteract the back bend. ▸ Relax down to the floor with your legs outstretched in front and arms to the side. Inhale, point your toes and bring your knees into your chest. Stretch your arms out in line with your shoulders. ▸ Exhale and take both knees to the right as you twist your spine to the left side and look over your left shoulder. ▸

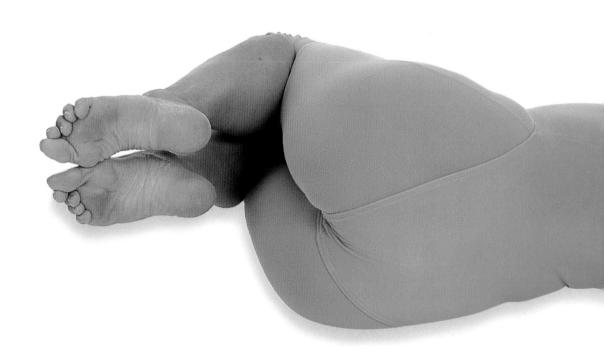

Inhale and return to the starting position. Exhale, take both knees to the left side and twist your spine and head to the right. Inhale and return to the starting position, then repeat the sequence.
▸ When you finish, draw your knees into your chest, pushing the small of your back on to the floor, keeping your head straight. ▸ Take your arms to your sides and push your palms down on the floor as you lift your legs up and over your head. ▸ Tuck your toes under to increase the stretch. Do not worry if you cannot reach the floor behind you. ▸ Hold on to your hips for support and with continued practice you will be able to stretch further backward. This motion stimulates the thyroid gland, which regulates the hormonal levels and metabolism in the body.
▸ Inhale and lift the left leg up in a straight line to the body. Exhale, relax the foot and breathe normally for 5–7 seconds. While you are holding the pose you will feel all the blood rush down the leg into the internal organs. This will replenish all the cells with a fresh blood supply. Lower the left leg and repeat on the other side. ▸

Slowly bend both legs and lower your knees to your forehead. ▸ When you reach a 90° angle to the floor, straighten your legs and hold the position, breathing deeply and evenly, for 10 seconds. Using the tummy muscles, slowly lower your legs to the floor. Relax. ▸ Turn over, place your hands directly under your shoulders and push your hips back so you are sitting on your heels. Stretch your arms out in front. Inhale and dive forward with your chest so

your hips are up and your chest is in line with your head. ▸ In a circular motion, lift your spine and look upward as you balance on your hands. ▸ Relax down to the floor. Bend both knees and take hold of your ankles. Place your chin on the floor. ▸ Inhale, lift your legs and head and balance on your hipbones. Exhale, then breathe deeply and evenly as you continue to stretch upward. Hold for 5 seconds then release slowly.

Day Four:
Opening the Chest

In yoga there are considered to be seven energy centres, or chakras, which relate to different parts of the body. These spinning wheels of energy must be flowing smoothly and evenly before a person can be balanced and centered, and this can only occur when the mind, body and soul are in total harmony and balance. The fourth chakra is related to the heart, which controls loving emotions. People who have suffered bad experiences will tend to close their heart to protect themselves from further pain. Opening the chest will help you to gain a more positive outlook on life in general; you will feel empowered and have the confidence to face the world with a brave heart.

Stand tall with your feet together. Take your arms up in front of your chest and bend your elbows, placing the right forearm over the left. Keep your arms level with your shoulders. ▶ Inhale, take your elbows back and open your chest. You will feel your shoulder blades moving toward each other. Exhale and return to the starting position. Repeat the exercise. ▶ Release your elbows and take your forearms in front of you in a parallel line with the palms facing toward each other. ▶ Inhale and take your elbows back as far as possible, palms facing forward. Exhale and return to the starting position. Repeat. ▶ Stand in perfect posture. Lift your chest upward while keeping your shoulders down. Inhale and lift your left knee up. Exhale, clasp both hands around your knee and draw your leg closer to your body. Breathing deeply, hold for 5 seconds. If you are unable to balance, lean your back against a wall or use a chair for assistance. ▶

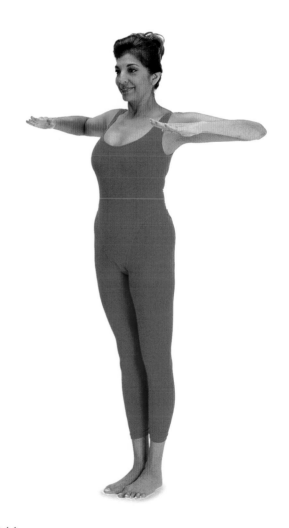

246

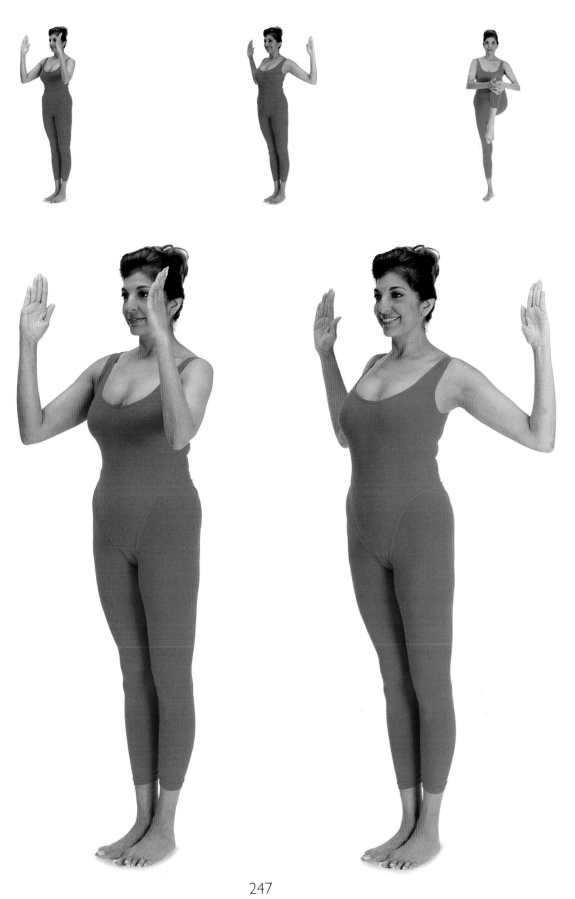

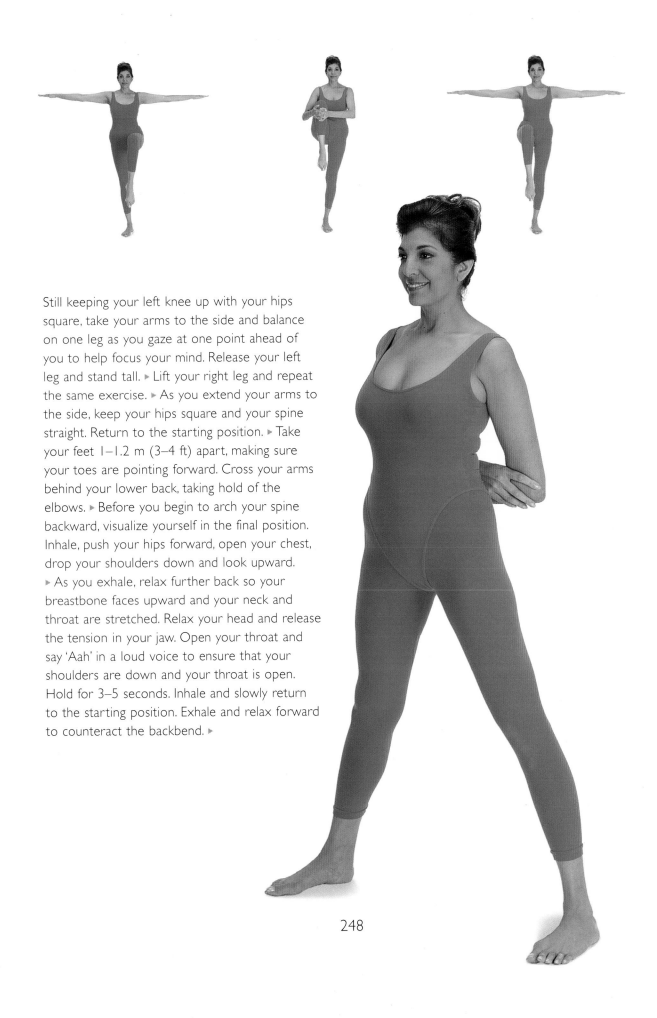

Still keeping your left knee up with your hips square, take your arms to the side and balance on one leg as you gaze at one point ahead of you to help focus your mind. Release your left leg and stand tall. ▸ Lift your right leg and repeat the same exercise. ▸ As you extend your arms to the side, keep your hips square and your spine straight. Return to the starting position. ▸ Take your feet 1–1.2 m (3–4 ft) apart, making sure your toes are pointing forward. Cross your arms behind your lower back, taking hold of the elbows. ▸ Before you begin to arch your spine backward, visualize yourself in the final position. Inhale, push your hips forward, open your chest, drop your shoulders down and look upward. ▸ As you exhale, relax further back so your breastbone faces upward and your neck and throat are stretched. Relax your head and release the tension in your jaw. Open your throat and say 'Aah' in a loud voice to ensure that your shoulders are down and your throat is open. Hold for 3–5 seconds. Inhale and slowly return to the starting position. Exhale and relax forward to counteract the backbend. ▸

248

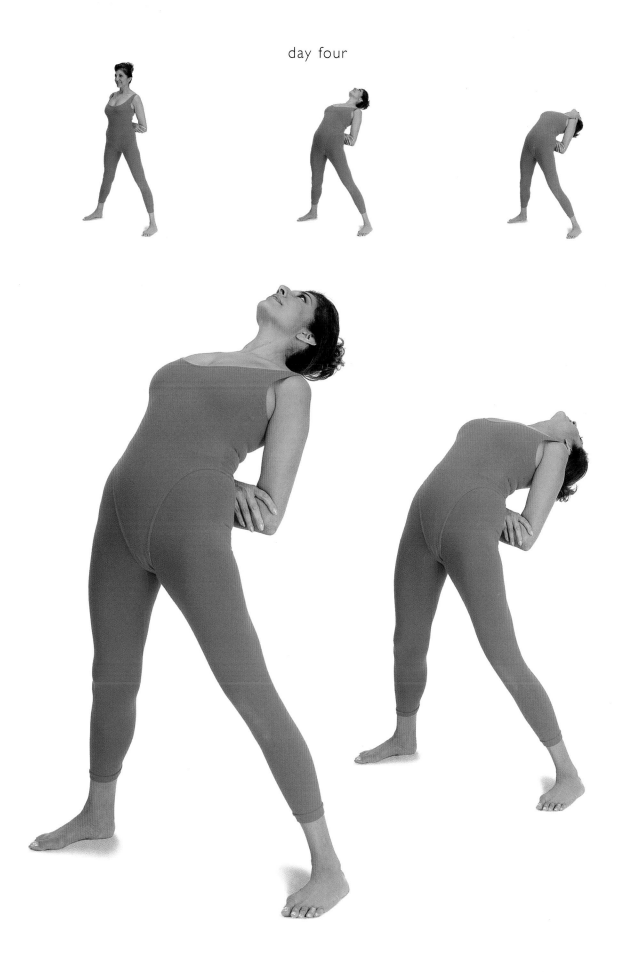

Standing tall, take your arms behind your lower back with your hands in a prayer position, fingertips facing up. This allows your chest to open even further. Turn your right foot to the right, making sure that your right heel is in a direct line to the instep of the left foot. Turn your torso completely to the right, trying to keep your hips square. ▸ Inhale, push your hips forward and drop your head back. Look upward, exhale, and breathe normally for 5 seconds. ▸ On the exhalation, drop your head forward toward your right knee, leading from the tail bone. Hold for 5 seconds. ▸ Inhale, tighten your tummy muscles and raise your torso until your head, back and hips are in a straight line. Exhale, breathe deeply and hold for 5 seconds. ▸ Bend your right knee in a 90° angle so the back of your knee is in a direct line to your right heel. Make sure you do not extend your knee over your foot. Inhale, straighten up, exhale and hold for 5 seconds, breathing normally. Repeat the entire sequence on the other side. Return to standing position. ▸ Lift your right leg up behind you, taking hold of the inside of your right foot. This helps keep the hips square. Take your left hand to your waist and hold until you have perfect balance. ▸

251

252

Focus your attention on a spot in front of you and begin to raise your right leg. ▸ Maintaining your balance, stretch even further, pointing your toe. Breathing deeply, hold for as long as possible, stretching in both directions. Repeat on the other side. ▸ Kneel on the floor, your knees in a direct line to your hips and arms behind your lower back. ▸ Pushing from your hips, arch backward. ▸ If you can, place your hands on your heels to increase the stretch. Continue to push your hips up, breathing deeply, and hold for 5–7 seconds. ▸ Sit on your heels and drop your head forward to counteract the pose. Lift your head and take your right arm over your right shoulder so your palm is facing your right shoulder blade. Take your left arm behind your back, palm facing outward. Inhale and try to clasp the palms together. Exhale, breathe normally and hold for 6 seconds. Repeat on the other side.

Day Five:
Energizing

Yoga is a form of exercise which constantly builds energy levels rather than depleting them. With advancing age there comes a drop in energy and some people believe that they should not do any form of exercise. Harsh and strenuous movements are harmful at any age but because yoga is very gentle on the joints even the very elderly can benefit. Try to keep the movements fluid and allow your whole body to move gracefully like a dancer. If you become short of breath during the series, take deeper breaths from the diaphragm to increase your energy flow. Repeat the section at least twice to feel the benefit and, at the end, bring your fingertips together to feel an exchange of energy from your right hand to your left.

This series of movements will energize your entire system, especially if you are feeling tired and lack energy to enjoy the pastimes you enjoy most. As you age it is more important to feel enthusiastic and full of vitality. Stand tall with your feet 1–1.2 m (3–4 ft) apart. Shift your weight to the left foot, lift the right heel off the floor and point the right foot and take both arms to the left. Extend your arms, palms facing each other, and stretch your body up, lifting your chest.
▸ Inhale and begin to swing your arms to the left in a wide circle. ▸ Bend your knees to increase the movement and take your arms down in front of you in a parallel line. ▸ Continue to swing your arms to the right and shift your weight to the right foot. ▸ As you bring your arms over to the left, exhale, and swing your body simultaneously to the left, completing the full circle. To increase the stretch, take the left arm out to the side. ▸

Curve your right arm in an angle to the right as you lift your left arm upward in a straight line. ▸ Stretch over to the right as far as possible and enjoy the feeling of moving the entire body as a whole. ▸ Curve the left arm and move the body toward the left. ▸ With a fluid, graceful motion, stretch over to the left as far as possible. Breathe normally as you move through the entire series. The stretching from side to side rejuvenates the whole body and lifts the spirit. Repeat the entire sequence. ▸ Stand tall with your feet 1–1.2 m (3–4 ft) apart, your toes pointing forward and arms outstretched to the side. Make sure your arms are in line with your shoulders with your palms facing down. ▸ Turn your left foot and swirl your body to the left, taking your left arm behind you and your right elbow in front of your chest. Twist from the waist as far as possible and make sure both arms are level with each other. ▸

Turn your right foot and swing your body and arms to the right. Return to standing position with your feet together. ▸ Keeping both hips square, raise your right knee and balance on your left foot. When you have perfect balance raise both arms over your head. Clasp your hands together and hold the position for 5 seconds. ▸ Breathing normally, take your right leg up and place your right foot on the inside of your left thigh. Make sure the standing leg is straight and lift the muscle above the kneecap to help you balance. Stretch your arms over your head, keeping your elbows straight. Cross your thumbs and place your palms together. Hold for 5 seconds. ▸ Release your arms, place your left hand on your waist and take your right hand down to your right foot. Clasp your first and second fingers around your big toe and flex your thumb. As you grab hold of your foot lean toward the right, keeping your spine erect. ▸ Inhale and stretch your leg out to the side as far as possible. Exhale, breathe normally and hold for 5 seconds. If you cannot extend the right leg fully, do not worry – it is more important to keep the hips square and the standing leg straight. ▸ Release your leg and place your feet 1–1.2 m (3–4 ft) apart. Turn your right foot to the right and bend your right knee. Place your hand on top of your knee with your fingers facing the inner thigh. ▸

258

Place your fingertips on the floor to the right.
▸ Inhale, bend your right knee further and at the
same time lift your left leg so it is in line with your
body. Exhale, flex the left foot and keep both legs
straight. Release to the last position on page 259.
Repeat on the other side. ▸ Kneel on the right knee
and take your left leg to the side. Take your right arm
up and place your left hand on your left knee.
▸ Inhale, stretch to the left and slide your hand to
your ankle. Exhale then, breathing deeply, hold for
7–10 seconds. Repeat on the other side. ▸ Sit on the
floor, bend your left knee and place your right foot
flat on the floor so your knee is up. Place both palms
on the floor to the left. ▸ Inhale, bend your left elbow
and lift your right leg up in a 90° angle to the floor.
Clasp the two first fingers around the big toe and flex
the thumb. Exhale, breathe normally and hold for
7–10 seconds. Repeat on the other side.

Day Six:
Rejuvenation

People who practice yoga always look younger than their years; their skin is clear, their eyes are bright and they seem to glow with well-being. The difference between yoga and other forms of exercise lies in the breathing techniques. *Pranayama*, or the science of breath, is the most important aspect of yoga philosophy. In this series of exercises, concentrate on breathing deeply and evenly throughout. When you inhale, fill your lungs completely from the diaphragm. Keep your shoulders down and don't raise your chest. The movement should be concentrated only on the lower abdomen. As you exhale, let the breath out slowly as you continue with the movement. This technique can be practiced on its own or used as a warm-up to any of the exercise routines.

Stand tall with your feet together. Interlace your fingers and place your hands under your chin. ▸ Inhale deeply and lift your elbows up as high as possible while keeping your head and chin level. ▸ Drop your head back, keeping your elbows up. ▸ Exhale through the mouth, blowing the air out slowly and evenly as you bring your elbows together. ▸ Inhale deeply, lift the elbows up in line with your shoulders and repeat the entire breathing exercise 7 times. Deepen the inhalation and exhalation as you continue this rejuvenating breathing technique. ▸

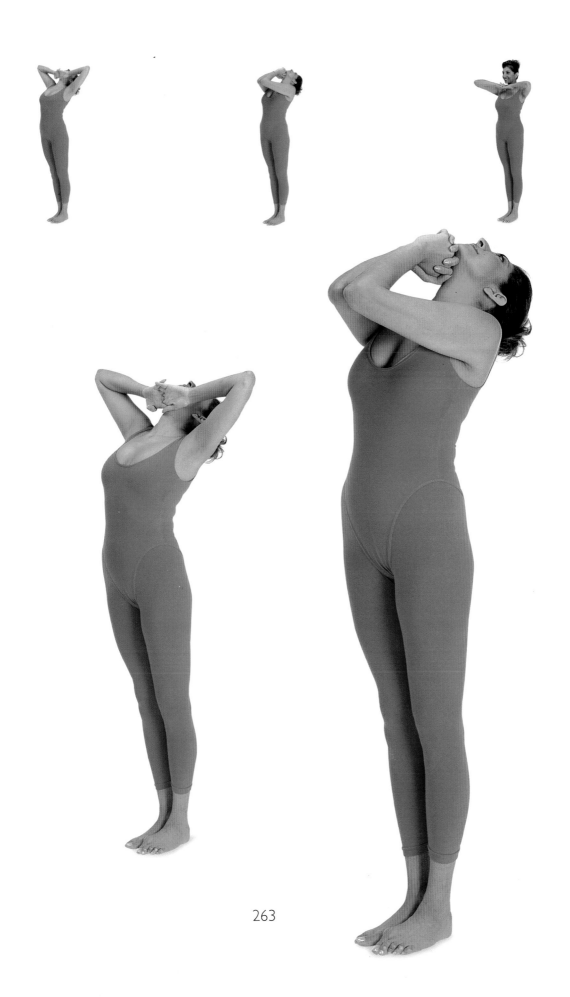

263

264

Inhale deeply and as you exhale slowly curve your spine, bend your elbows and drop your head forward, looking down to your fingertips. ▸ With a flowing movement, stretch your spine down and straighten your arms. Face your palms down toward your feet and let the natural weight of your body extend your spine further down. ▸ Inhale deeply and sweep your arms forward in a circular motion. Keep your head between your arms as you take your arms up over your head. ▸ Drop your head back and look up to your fingertips. Breathe deeply and evenly. Hold for 5 seconds. ▸ Straighten your head, bring your palms together and continue to stretch your arms up. Make sure your shoulders are down and your head is locked between your elbows. ▸ Keeping your spine straight, bend your knees, keeping your toes and heels firmly on the floor. Breathing deeply, hold for 5 seconds. ▸

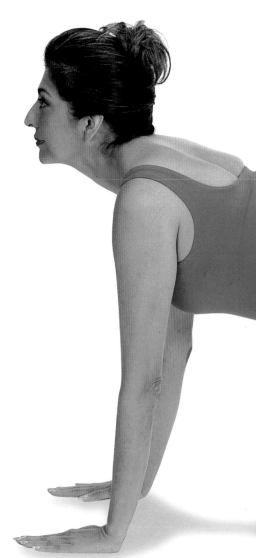

Pull your tummy muscles in and take your hips back, keeping your spine straight. ▸ Breathing deeply, bend your knees further, shift your weight to your heels and take your hips back into a sitting position. Hold for 10 seconds. Return to standing position. ▸ Kneel down, knees directly under your hips, and place your palms on the floor beneath your shoulders. Inhale, curl your spine forward and simultaneously bring your right knee up toward your forehead. ▸ Exhale and swing your right leg back and up. Point your right foot. Inhale and bring your right knee back to your forehead. Exhale and return to kneeling position. Repeat on the other side.

▸ Lie on the floor. Place your forearms on the floor and lift your head slightly. ▸ Inhale, push down, straighten your elbows and lift your spine. Keep your hipbones down and gaze upward. Exhale, breathe normally and hold for 7–10 seconds. ▸

266

day six

Lie flat on the floor. Bring your knees up directly in line with your hips. Put your palms together and stretch your arms over your head. ▶ Inhale and as you exhale tighten your tummy muscles and bring your hands over your head to your knees, slowly lifting your head and shoulders off the floor. ▶ Sitting up further, inhale and raise your arms above your knees. ▶ Exhale, lower your back halfway down to the floor and bring your arms up in a straight line to your shoulders. ▶ Inhale and take your arms over your head as you slowly lower your spine to the floor. Exhale and lower your arms to the floor. ▶ Inhale, bend your elbows and bring your hands over the top of your head, palms together. Repeat the entire series 5 times. Keep the breathing pattern fluid as you move from one position to the next. Hold your breath for 2 seconds in each position to gain breath control.

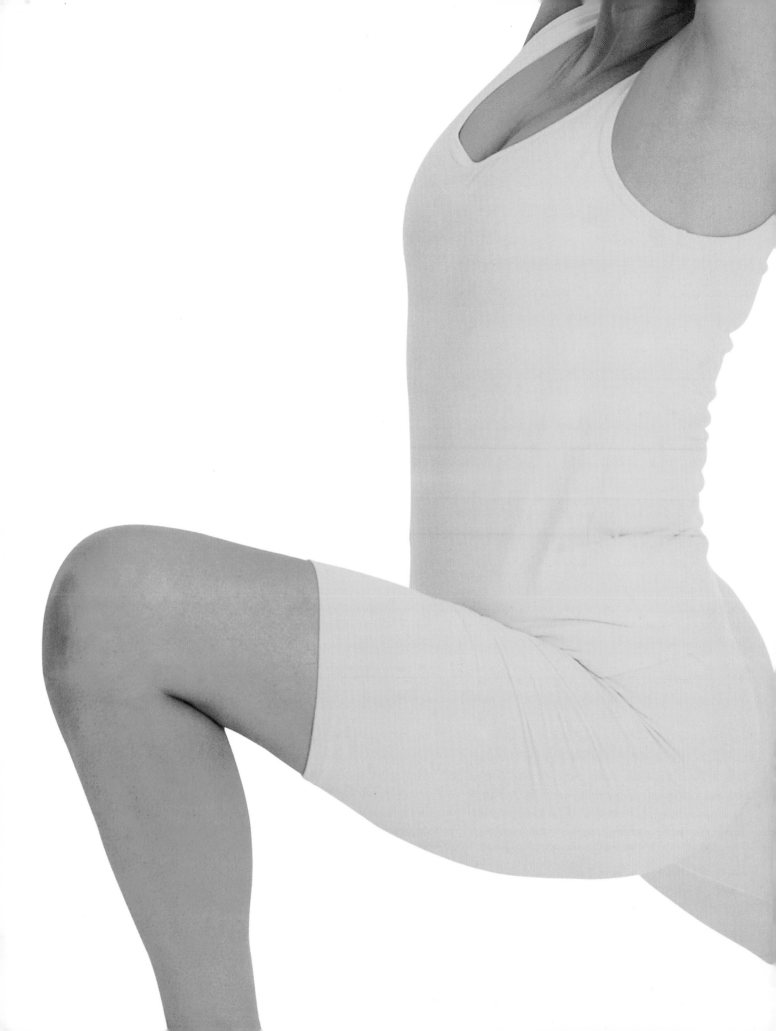

Maintenance

The positions on pages 272–7 constitute an exercise plan that tones and lifts the specific muscle groups that show the first signs of ageing. If your body is losing its elasticity and your muscles are beginning to sag it is important to address the problem before it becomes severe – but it is better still to keep yourself in shape and use this plan as a preventive measure. These exercises are designed to lift the entire body to restore youthfulness and suppleness; they will tone the ankles, calves, kneecaps and upper thighs, flatten the tummy, lift the buttocks and reduce the hips and waist. It is a dynamic fitness routine that can be done on its own or for increased benefit can be combined with any Day plan, depending on how much time you have or what specific areas you need to work on.

This fitness routine can also be a preface to the Remedial exercises which appear in the latter half of this section. Because the Remedial section targets specific problem areas, you will notice the results in a surprisingly short time. Doctors now agree that there is a direct link between the emotional balance of a person and their susceptibility to certain illnesses – people suffering from stomach cramps, for example, are often emotionally upset. They commonly take medication to relieve their pain, but yoga will relax the stomach cramps immediately because it teaches you to breathe through the pain in order to release it. Because yoga tones, reoxygenates and rejuvenates the entire body, it can alleviate a whole range of common problems, both physical and mental.

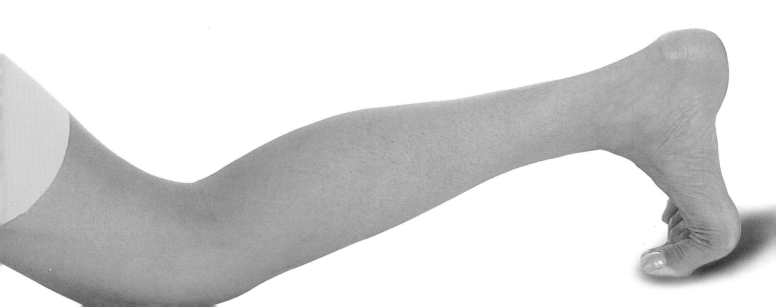

Stomach Stretches

This series of movements will tighten and tone the lower abdominal muscles and flatten the tummy. Pay extra attention to the breathing pattern for the best results; breathing incorrectly may even build the muscles so your tummy actually appears larger.

Lie flat on the floor with your arms to the side. Bring your left knee up and place your left foot flat on the floor. Point your right foot and take both arms over your head. Place your palms together and straighten your elbows. ▸ Inhale and lift your right leg up to a 90° angle. Exhale, breathe normally and hold for 5 seconds. ▸ Inhale and bring your palms in toward your head. Exhale, sit up and bring your arms down in front of your face above the chest. ▸ Inhale, straighten your arms, exhale, breathe normally and hold for 5 seconds. Inhale, slowly lower your back and take your arms over your head. ▸ Exhale, lower your right leg, then your left and repeat the exercise on the other side.

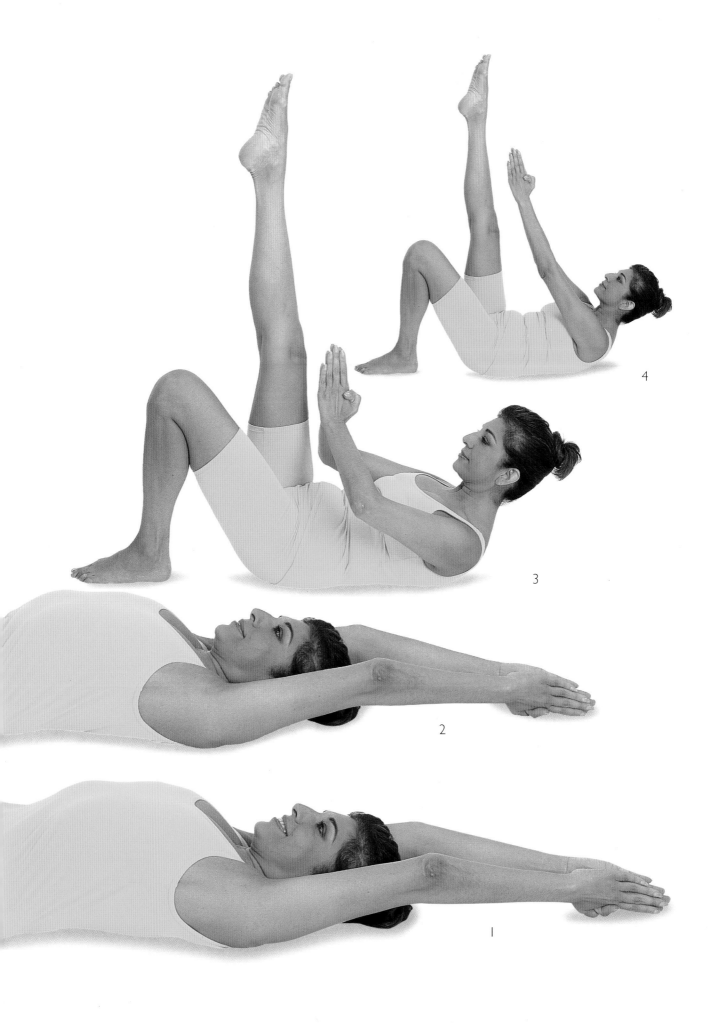

4

3

2

1

Push-ups

2

3

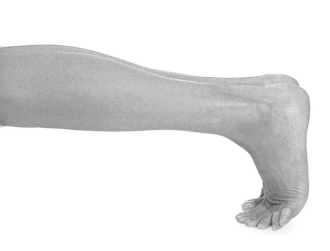

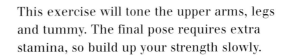

This exercise will tone the upper arms, legs and tummy. The final pose requires extra stamina, so build up your strength slowly.

Sit back on your heels, tuck your toes under and stretch your arms out in front of you with your palms facing down. Leaving your hands in the same place, bend your elbows and push your palms down to the floor. Your arms will take the weight of your body as you do the next movement. ▸ Inhale, bring your chin down toward the floor and curve your spine down and up in a beautiful arch. Exhale, point your toes, straighten your elbows and lift your hips off the floor. Make sure you keep your shoulders down. Breathing normally, hold the pose for 5 seconds. ▸ Tuck your toes under and lift your whole body off the floor. Balance on your hands and feet and make sure your weight is evenly distributed between the two. Hold for 5 seconds. When you feel that you have the strength, inhale, bend your elbows and bring your entire body down to 7.5cm (3 inches) from the floor. Exhale, extend your arms and hold for 5 seconds. Repeat.

Table Top

This exercise will tone every muscle simultaneously and requires flexibility, strength and stamina. It will help to focus your mind and give you a feeling of inner harmony. It is a challenging pose so it might take you some time and practice to master it.

Sit down with your legs outstretched in front of you. Point your toes, leave your feet flat down and bring your knees slightly off the floor in line with your waist. Lean back and take your arms behind you so your hands are hip-width apart and your fingers are facing your body. ▶ Straighten your arms, tighten your tummy and buttock muscles, inhale and lift your whole body off the floor. ▶ Exhale, inhale, and to increase the stretch, contract your buttock muscles and lift your hips higher off the floor so your body is in a perfect diagonal line. Exhale and drop your head back. Breathe normally and hold this intense stretch for 5–7 seconds. To release, sit back down on the floor.

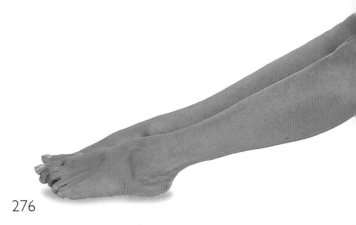

276

2

3

Remedial
Arthritis

This exercise is excellent for relieving stiffness in the joints. At first it might feel uncomfortable but continued practice will alleviate the pain and increase circulation to the joints.

Kneel up tall then tuck the toes under and sit back on to the heels. If you feel any pain release the toes and continue. ▸ Place your hands behind you for support, fingers pointing away from you. Keep your arms and spine straight. Breathing normally, lift your hips up and push them forward as high as possible while balancing on your hands. Your weight should be evenly distributed between your arms and hips. ▸ Drop your head back, lifting your chin and hips up to create a circular shape with your spine. Hold for at least 5 seconds and repeat. When you are able to hold this pose comfortably, increase to 10 seconds.

1

2

3

Osteoporosis

As you age your bones become brittle without extra calcium and a good supply of blood to the hip area. This twist sends fresh oxygen and a purified blood supply to the hips and increases the circulation of the entire system. It alleviates painful conditions like sciatica as well as strengthening the hip joints.

Stand tall with your feet 1–1.2 m (3–4 ft) apart. Turn your left foot to the left and make sure your left heel is in a direct line with the instep of your right foot. Take your arms out to the side in line with your shoulders. Bend your right elbow so it is in line with your left knee. ▶ Inhale, put your right hand on the floor, exhale, twist your spine and look up over your left shoulder. Breathe deeply and hold for 5–7 seconds. Keep your arms in a straight line. If you are unable to touch the floor with your hand hold any part of your left leg. Repeat on the other side.

2

1

Immune System

Stress weakens the immune system and makes the body vulnerable to all kinds of health problems. It is hard to eliminate stress from our lives but we *can* boost the immune system in order to prevent ailments from becoming chronic.

Sit sideways on the floor, leaning on your right hip. Straighten your right leg and point your toe. Take your left knee up so your left foot is flat on the floor behind the right knee. Place your right palm on the floor about 30cm (1ft) from your right hip. Place your left hand near the upper thigh of your right leg. ▶ Inhale and push yourself up, balancing on your right hand and right foot. Exhale, keeping the legs parallel and your right arm fully extended. Your left arm should be pointed straight up in the air in line with your right arm. Breathe deeply and hold for as long as you can. Repeat on the other side.

1

2

Thyroid

This exercise keeps the thyroid stabilized and helps with menopausal symptoms.

Lie flat on the floor, legs outstretched. Inhale and bring the knees to the chest. Exhale, push your palms down on the floor and roll your legs over your head. Breathe normally and hold your lower back to support your weight. Take your knees to the floor on either side of your head, close to your ears. ▸ Tighten your tummy muscles, place the soles of your feet together and create a triangle with your legs. ▸ Inhale, straighten your legs, tighten your buttock muscles and point your toes. Breathing deeply, hold for 20 seconds. To release, slowly bend your knees toward your forehead. Lower your spine, pushing each vertebra down to the floor. Lower your legs to the floor and relax for 20 seconds.

3

2

I

Depression

1

Our mental state affects us physically, so it is vital to keep a positive outlook. This is not always easy, but keeping the mind alert and the body mobile will prevent depression. When you are in this inverted position the blood rushes to the brain and nourishes the cells.

Kneel on the floor, tuck your toes under and sit on your heels. Interlace your fingers, make a triangle with your arms and place your elbows under your shoulders. ▶ Place the top of your head on the floor, fingertips touching the back of your head. Inhale, straighten your legs and balance on your toes.
▶ Exhale, push your shoulders down and straighten your spine. Breathing normally, hold for 5 seconds. Bend your knees to the floor. Hold for 5 seconds and repeat, this time holding for 10 seconds. Sit back on your heels, your forehead on the floor. Relax for a few moments and lift your head slowly.

2

3

Eye Strain

As people age the eye muscles become lax. These exercises are designed to strengthen the eye muscles so vision is improved.

Sit up tall in a comfortable cross-legged position. Straighten your index finger and place it in front of your nose. Stretch your right arm out in front of you and stare at your finger for 5 seconds. ▶ Keeping your eyes focused on your finger, slowly bring it toward you until it touches the tip of your nose. Still keeping your eyes focused on your finger, stretch the arm out again. Rub your hands and place your palms over your eyes. ▶ Keeping your head straight, take your arm up to the right, eyes still focused on your finger. ▶ Then take your arm diagonally to the left. Repeat on the same side, then on the other side. Rub your hands together and cup them over your eyes.

1

2

3

4

Pelvic Floor

1

2

After childbirth and with advancing age, many women suffer from incontinence and other urinary disorders. The pelvic floor must be kept toned in order for the urinary system and sexual organs to function properly. As you do the following exercise, contract the pelvic muscle to bring elasticity to the vaginal wall, which will increase sensation during sexual intercourse.

Lie face down on the floor, arms to the side. Place your elbows under the shoulder blades with your palms face down and your fingers together. Inhale, push your palms and elbows down and lift your head up. Make sure your hipbones remain on the floor. Exhale and point your toes. ▸ Breathing normally, lift both legs up behind you, keeping your feet together. ▸ Balancing on your right arm, reach back with your left hand and take hold of your left foot. Lift your spine and look up. Hold for 5–7 seconds. Repeat on the other side.

3

Breaks and Fractures

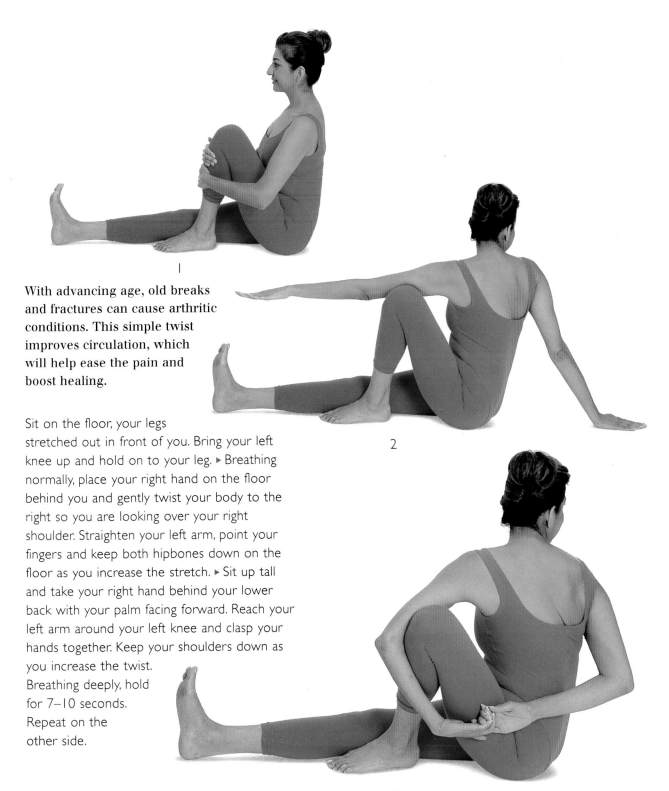

1

With advancing age, old breaks and fractures can cause arthritic conditions. This simple twist improves circulation, which will help ease the pain and boost healing.

Sit on the floor, your legs stretched out in front of you. Bring your left knee up and hold on to your leg. ▸ Breathing normally, place your right hand on the floor behind you and gently twist your body to the right so you are looking over your right shoulder. Straighten your left arm, point your fingers and keep both hipbones down on the floor as you increase the stretch. ▸ Sit up tall and take your right hand behind your lower back with your palm facing forward. Reach your left arm around your left knee and clasp your hands together. Keep your shoulders down as you increase the twist. Breathing deeply, hold for 7–10 seconds. Repeat on the other side.

2

Index

First published in Great Britain in 1999 by
Hamlyn, a division of Octopus Publishing Group Ltd,
2-4 Heron Quays, London, E14 4JP

Reprinted 2001

Pages 16–32 of Text © Octopus Publishing Group Ltd
1999, 2001
All other Text © The Natural Therapy Company
Limited 1999, 2001
Design © Octopus Publishing Group Limited 1999
Photographs © Octopus Publishing Group Limited 1999

ISBN 0 600 60567 1

A CIP catalogue record of this book is available from
the British Library.

Printed and bound in China

The textual material in this book is an abridged version
of the following titles previously published by Hamlyn:
Yogacise (1994); *Classic Yoga* (1995); *Yoga for Stress*
(1997); *Yoga for Sex* (1997); *Stop the Age Clock* (1998).

ACKNOWLEDGEMENTS

Operations Director: Alison Goff
Executive Editor: Jane McIntosh
Project Editor: Catharine Davey
Editor: Diana Vowles
Creative Director: Keith Martin
Design Manager: Bryan Dunn
Jacket Design: Leigh Jones/Anna Pow
Designer: Stephen Cary
Photography: John Adriaan
            Gary Houlder
            Tim Ridley
Production Controller: Sarah Scanlon

JACKET PHOTOGRAPHY

Octopus Publishing Group Ltd/Tim Ridley

£5.99

© 2000 Bluenet Limited

Written by Teresa Maughan

Designed by Jason Bazini

Published in Great Britain in 2000
by Egmont World Limited,
a division of Egmont Holding Limite
Deanway Technology Centre,
Wilmslow Road, Handforth,
Cheshire, SK9 3FB, UK.
Printed in Italy. ISBN 0 7498 5034

westlife

contents

Nicky

Mark

Well, would you believe it? Five Irish guys on top of the world, and it's all down to you! It's been a fantastic couple of

Bryan

Kian

Shane

years for us, and we're
so grateful to you, our
loyal fans, who have
helped us live our dream.
**Enjoy the book, and
see you soon!**

That's 'Life'

Westlife's rapid rise to fame is one of the most spectacular in pop. Hold tight!

It's true what they say about the luck of the Irish. Not content with producing one fab boy band, Boyzone, the Emerald Isle is responsible for another group of talented young lads who make up pop's biggest sensation this century — Westlife. So, how did the saucy smoochers get together — and has their rise to the top been meteoric or a long, hard battle?

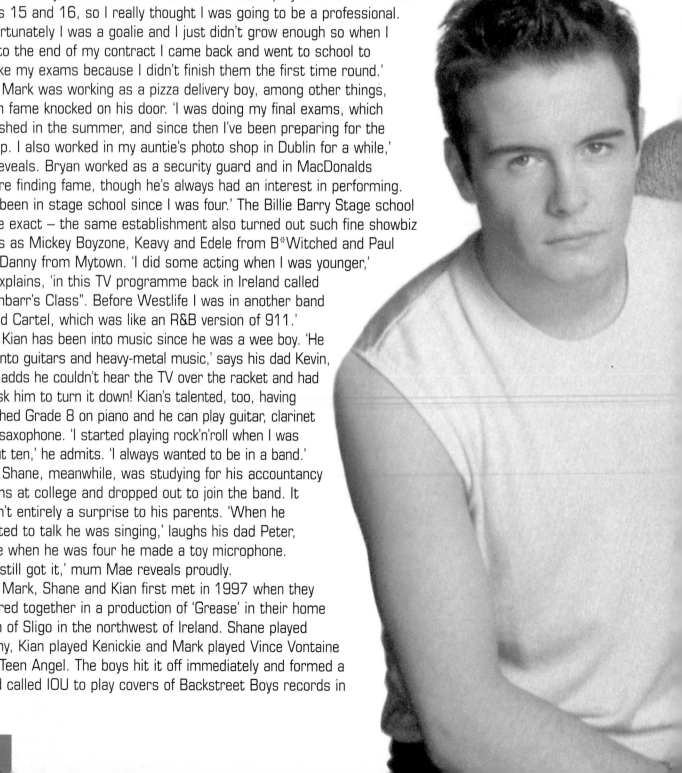

Just two and a half years ago life for the fab five was very different as the boys themselves reveal. 'I was playing football for Leeds United,' explains Nicky, 'which was a dream come true. I played for Ireland when I was 15 and 16, so I really thought I was going to be a professional. Unfortunately I was a goalie and I just didn't grow enough so when I got to the end of my contract I came back and went to school to retake my exams because I didn't finish them the first time round.'

Mark was working as a pizza delivery boy, among other things, when fame knocked on his door. 'I was doing my final exams, which I finished in the summer, and since then I've been preparing for the group. I also worked in my auntie's photo shop in Dublin for a while,' he reveals. Bryan worked as a security guard and in MacDonalds before finding fame, though he's always had an interest in performing. 'I've been in stage school since I was four.' The Billie Barry Stage school to be exact — the same establishment also turned out such fine showbiz stars as Mickey Boyzone, Keavy and Edele from B*Witched and Paul and Danny from Mytown. 'I did some acting when I was younger,' he explains, 'in this TV programme back in Ireland called "46inbarr's Class". Before Westlife I was in another band called Cartel, which was like an R&B version of 911.'

Kian has been into music since he was a wee boy. 'He got into guitars and heavy-metal music,' says his dad Kevin, who adds he couldn't hear the TV over the racket and had to ask him to turn it down! Kian's talented, too, having reached Grade 8 on piano and he can play guitar, clarinet and saxophone. 'I started playing rock'n'roll when I was about ten,' he admits. 'I always wanted to be in a band.'

Shane, meanwhile, was studying for his accountancy exams at college and dropped out to join the band. It wasn't entirely a surprise to his parents. 'When he started to talk he was singing,' laughs his dad Peter, while when he was four he made a toy microphone. 'I've still got it,' mum Mae reveals proudly.

Mark, Shane and Kian first met in 1997 when they starred together in a production of 'Grease' in their home town of Sligo in the northwest of Ireland. Shane played Danny, Kian played Kenickie and Mark played Vince Vontaine and Teen Angel. The boys hit it off immediately and formed a band called IOU to play covers of Backstreet Boys records in

That's 'Life'

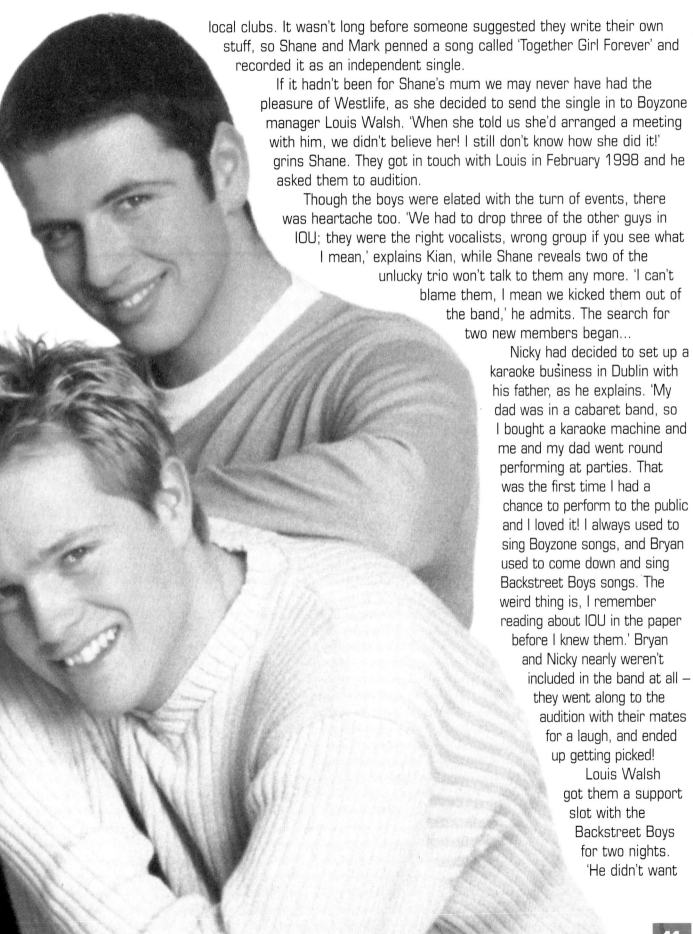

local clubs. It wasn't long before someone suggested they write their own stuff, so Shane and Mark penned a song called 'Together Girl Forever' and recorded it as an independent single.

If it hadn't been for Shane's mum we may never have had the pleasure of Westlife, as she decided to send the single in to Boyzone manager Louis Walsh. 'When she told us she'd arranged a meeting with him, we didn't believe her! I still don't know how she did it!' grins Shane. They got in touch with Louis in February 1998 and he asked them to audition.

Though the boys were elated with the turn of events, there was heartache too. 'We had to drop three of the other guys in IOU; they were the right vocalists, wrong group if you see what I mean,' explains Kian, while Shane reveals two of the unlucky trio won't talk to them any more. 'I can't blame them, I mean we kicked them out of the band,' he admits. The search for two new members began...

Nicky had decided to set up a karaoke business in Dublin with his father, as he explains. 'My dad was in a cabaret band, so I bought a karaoke machine and me and my dad went round performing at parties. That was the first time I had a chance to perform to the public and I loved it! I always used to sing Boyzone songs, and Bryan used to come down and sing Backstreet Boys songs. The weird thing is, I remember reading about IOU in the paper before I knew them.' Bryan and Nicky nearly weren't included in the band at all – they went along to the audition with their mates for a laugh, and ended up getting picked! Louis Walsh got them a support slot with the Backstreet Boys for two nights. 'He didn't want

That's 'Life'

to manage us because he was so busy with Boyzone,' reveals Kian. 'Once he saw us on stage though, he changed his mind. So we brought in Nicky and Bryan, changed our name to Westside and took it from there.' But they weren't to be called Westside for long as it became clear there were other bands with the same name abroad, so they changed their name to Westlife and a pop phenomenon was born.

Getting a record deal proved to be just as easy too. RCA/BMG A&R chief (and talent scout) Simon Cowell took just 30 seconds to make up his mind after hearing them singing on stage. 'It's the only time it's ever happened. I knew instantly this was absolutely the band I wanted to work with in 1999 and what I wanted to do with them. They looked great and sounded amazing.'

Kian recalls their first encounter with just as much enthusiasm. 'As soon as we met Simon everyone just clicked. He knew the sound we were looking for and how to go image-wise. And he was 100 per cent honest with us. Other labels would say that's great and we'd not hear from them – but he wanted it straight away. We trust him, and so does Louis. It's his job to get the music. We will do absolutely anything if he suggests it. He put his whole energy into us.'

In April of 1998 Louis Walsh offered Boyzone heart-throb Ronan Keating the chance to be involved with Westlife on a co-management basis. 'I wanted to help the lads and give them the chance Louis gave me five years ago,' he reveals. 'They had what we had four years ago – the hunger and spark. There's no reason they can't be the biggest boy band in the world.' Ronan clearly knew what he was talking about, because it would be less than a year before Westlife would take the charts by storm coming straight in at Number 1 with their first single... but more of that later!

Then began the relentless touring beginning with a summer tour with Boyzone and culminating with the Smash Hits Tour and Poll Winners' Party where the boys would pick up the magazine's coveted award for best new tour act of '98. 'That was a high point,' says Kian. 'Ronan said "Smash Hits is where it all started for Boyzone, and hopefully it'll happen for you as well. Just work hard and you'll be OK." So we are keeping our fingers crossed,' Shane confessed. 'We can't wait to be the biggest pop group ever.' Well they certainly wouldn't have to wait long...

Bryan

Name:	Bryan Nicholas McFadden
Date of birth:	12 April 1980
Place of birth:	Dublin
Lives now:	Artane, Dublin
Colour of eyes:	Blue
Colour of hair:	Light brown/blond
Height:	6ft 1in
Hobbies:	Singing, dancing, music and football
Likes:	Music, females and spending money
Dislikes:	School, reading, writing, other people's sadness – he likes everybody to be happy
Fave sport:	Soccer
Fave actor:	Leo DiCaprio
Fave actress:	Jennifer Love Hewitt
Best movie ever:	*Titanic*
Fave place to chill:	On the beach or on a boat
Fave place to visit:	USA
Fave one-liner:	How're ya, Love?

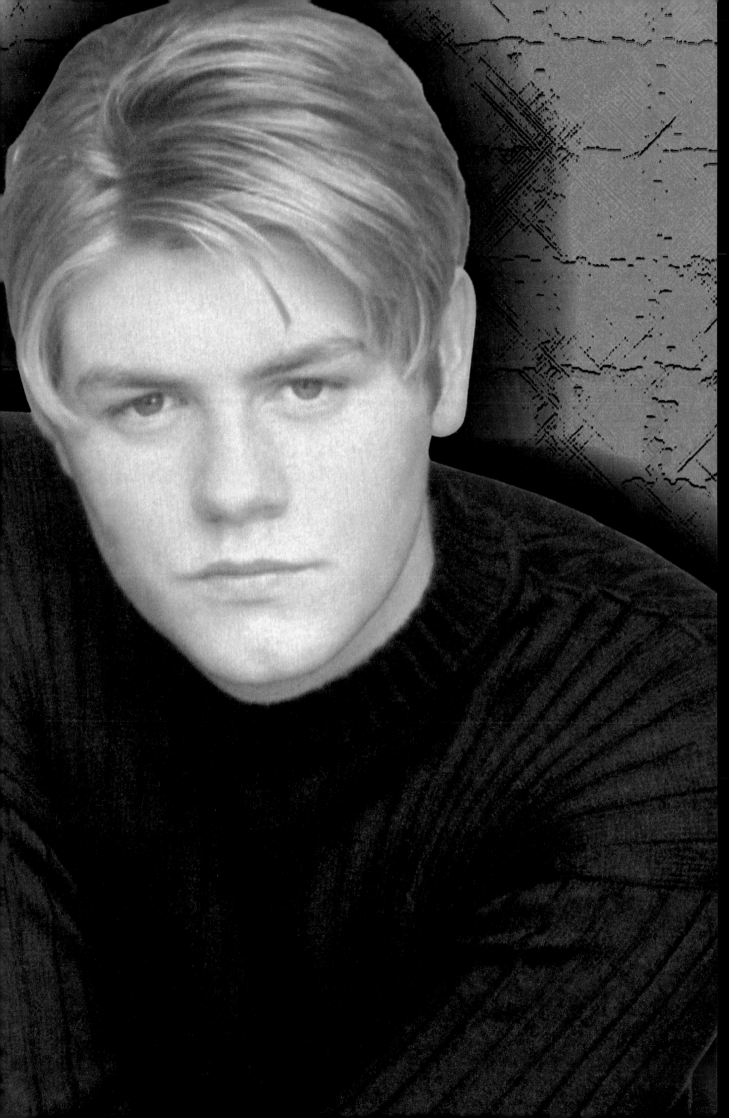

Family 'Life'

The Westlifers are homeboys, and never fail to return to their families at every opportunity. We find out why they're so attached to the folks back home.

Mark

Family: Mum Marie, dad Oliver, brothers Barry (14) and Colin (9)
Pets: Horses – Star, Freddy, Charlie and Jenny; Dog – Black Labrador called Sloopy

Mark's definitely a home-loving bod and nips back to Sligo whenever he can. 'I talk to my parents every day on the phone,' he reveals. 'I'm very close to everyone back home in Sligo.' He misses them desperately when he's away and spends a fortune on mobile phone calls. 'He always rings two or three times a day and he still likes to go out with his dad, Barry and Colin when he comes home,' says mum, Marie.

His family are obviously proud of him and would have supported him whatever he had chosen to do. 'He was a brilliant young lad at school, very bright, very intelligent,' coos mum. 'Mark was a busy baby, always active and climbing everywhere. It was hard to make him sleep – we had to put a radio beside his cot,' remembers dad, Oliver.

His love of music began at an early age when, on the last day of playschool the teacher had a concert. 'All the other children sang their nursery rhyme but Mark stood up and sang "Uptown Girl" by Billy Joel,' recalls mum. 'Every evening you'd hear Mark walking down the road from school playing his penny whistle,' says dad. 'He still locks himself in the bathroom and all you can hear is singing.'

Despite his fame Mark still has his feet firmly glued to the (bathroom) floor. 'He still does his own ironing. I experienced that on his last break,' says mum. 'He was getting ready to go out for the night and his black shirt wasn't ironed but he said, "Give it to me, mum, I'll do that." So he still partakes in a few household chores.'

Mark loves his family to bits too. 'They've always been there right from the start. They're the nicest bunch of people in the world. My mum's such a bubbly person and she's always in a good mood. My dad is always going out of his way to help. They're both really good-natured people. My little brother is a happy-go-lucky young fella

Family 'Life'

who doesn't have a care in the world, except when it comes to football, and Barry reminds me so much of myself at his age 'cos I was really shy too,' he says.

So what do his family think of his fame? 'We get very emotional and worked up when we see Mark on the telly but we're getting used to it. Mark's done us proud,' says dad. 'We always get a call from Mark afterwards asking, "Well, how did it go?" I'll say, "You looked fine." I always reassure him,' says mum. With support like that, how can he fail?

Shane

Family: Mum Mae, dad Peter, brothers Finbarr (30), Peter (29), Liam (27), sisters Yvonne (28), Denise (23) and Mairead (21)

Pets: German Shepherd dog called Kaiser and loads of horses

Shane's family are a close-knit one and run a family restaurant in his home town of Sligo. 'Shane's worked here at the restaurant with us since he was five until about two years ago,' says dad Peter. 'When he was really young he'd run messages but when he was older he'd be here virtually every summer. He worked every night, often till two in the morning. Even now he's in Westlife, when he comes home he's still standing here behind the chip counter the same as ever.' Shane is the youngest of seven and reckons he's been well looked after. 'I was spoilt; with six elder brothers and sisters, everyone looked after me.'

His mum and dad never had any doubts that he would be a success. 'I always knew he'd do something, whether it was acting or singing, but I never thought it would happen so quickly for him,' admits his mum. 'Shane was into show-jumping, football and rugby when he was a child. When he was eight years old he won a kick-boxing contest,' she recalls. 'He took part acting in lots of shows and that's where he met Kian and Mark,' recalls dad.

Shane's parents have fifty horses, and there's nothing he likes better than donning his jodhpurs and saddling up for a canter on horseback when he goes home. He misses his family when he's away and reckons he owes everything to them. 'My mum is the whole reason I'm doing this job. She's supported me throughout my life and guided me. My dad's the same and we sometimes have man-to-man chats. I'd like to say thank you to my parents for bringing me up the right way. They're the best.' Awwww!

Nicky

Family: Mum Yvonne, dad Nicky, brother Adam (8) and sister Gillian (23)

Pets: None

Nicky had a happy childhood and was a bit of a charmer even as a wee lad – mum Yvonne dishes the dirt. 'Nicky was shy when he was younger and liked to go to bed early but he was a happy child. From the age of about six he always had the teachers under his thumb. He was very popular with everyone at school and got a fair few Valentine's cards from the girls.'

Nicky senior recalls his son's sporting talents fondly. 'He loves snooker and he's crazy about fishing. We once went out, me with my battered old rod held together with elastic bands and him with his fancy fishing rod. I caught seven mackerel and he caught nothing!'

Nicky wasn't always fond of music, as his mum reveals. 'When he was 15 he didn't want to sing in his exams – but his music teacher Mrs Murphy was having none of it and thankfully he passed with honours.' When he returned home from Leeds, his dad helped him in the karaoke business where he discovered his love for performing.

Though Nicky loves being in Westlife, he really misses home. 'On his first night away I got back from shopping to find out Nicky had been on the phone... reality had set in and he'd had a cry,' says mum. 'He's a worrier. It took him a while to settle into his new lifestyle. He still phones me every day.' Nicky knows he is lucky to have such a special family. 'I was very, very lucky to have the best childhood ever. I never went without anything. My parents are great people. Dad's really easy-going and mum's always on the phone to me.'

Bryan

Family: Mum Mairead, dad Brendan and sister Susan (16)

Pets: A Shih Tzu dog called Chip

Bryan was a bit of a wild child when he was a nipper as his mum, Mairead, reveals. 'Bryan was always into everything, climbing trees and counter tops. I never had a problem with him but he was cheeky and very loveable.'

Once when his mum was heavily pregnant with sister Susan, Bryan, then aged three, ran away from his mum in a shopping centre. 'He knew I couldn't run fast and he just kept looking back

Family 'Life'

and laughing at me. The more he ran the more he laughed. Luckily I eventually caught up with him and grabbed him by his hair.'

His father remembers a boy obsessed with Sylvester Stallone films. 'He loved football and "Rocky" films. He played those over and over until the tapes were worn out!' His dad also recalls Bryan's love of riding a tractor whenever they went on a farm. He's always been a dare-devil too. 'Bryan fears nothing. He used to jump off a big drop called Harry's Hole into the sea when we were on holiday and scare us to death,' recalls his mum.

Like the other 'Lifers Bryan adores his family. 'My mam is crazy! She's really, really funny and she's got loads of energy. She's very special. My dad is very quiet when you first meet him but when you get to know him you'll find he loves a good joke. He's also very kind. My sister Susan is a sweetheart and I love her to bits. She's very quiet and shy and she's a lovely girl.'

Kian

Family: Mum Patricia, dad Kevin, sisters Viv (29), Fenelir (24), Marielle (13), brothers Gavin (28), Tom (22), Colm (5)
Pets: None

According to his mum, Patricia, Kian has always been a man of action and his dad Kevin, agrees. 'He's always been a leader right from a kid.' He also enjoyed dressing up and prancing about. 'He once had to dress as a skeleton for a school play. He insisted I use the exact number of ribs in the correct place on his costume. I had to look it up in a medical book,' laughs his mum.

Kian was always keen on music, especially rock. 'When he was growing up he'd sing around the house,' remembers his dad. He learnt piano up to Grade 8 and loads of other instruments, but unbelievably the ladies' man of the band didn't look at females in his early days. 'Kian never liked girls when he was younger.' But that's changed now,' admits mum. 'We get loads of fan mail every day – each time he comes home there's another 200 letters for him to open. They are from all over the world.'

His family are chuffed to bits that he's found success so young. 'It was absolutely fabulous, totally unbelievable to hear my lad on the radio,' enthuses dad proudly. 'We were delighted.'

At the end of the day, though, home is where Kian's heart is. 'I love mum to bits just for being my mum. She's very supportive in everything I do and she got me into

music in a big way. My dad's a great guy. He taught me to play golf and he worked really hard to pay for the things I wanted like my guitars. My dad's quiet and when he comes home he likes to sit in front of the TV with the remote, you know, be the man of the house. Mum's always in the kitchen running around tidying things up – just like any mum, I s'pose.'

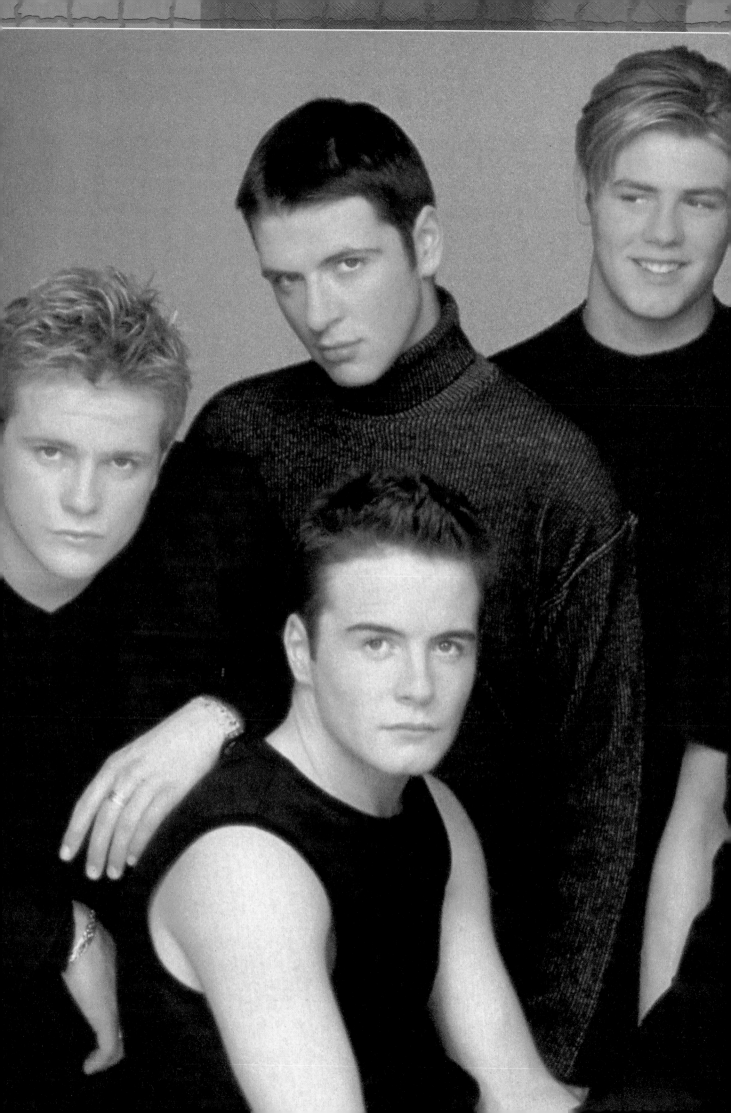

Boys will be boys

One minute the five lads from Westlife were ordinary boys living at home with their folks in Ireland and the next they're jet-setting around the world leading the life of Riley. Has their new lifestyle gone to their heads or are they still the same fellas?

Lads are often a bit of a handful when they get their first taste of freedom and can get themselves into trouble if they're not careful. But what happens when your first flirtation with the outside world comes as a member of one of the world's biggest boy bands? Luckily the Westlife boys are a down-to earth bunch, who like having fun, but know where to draw the line. Bryan admits that he smashed up a wardrobe in a hotel room once while on tour, but 'I was wrestling with the other lads and it was an accident.' Kian claims Westlife aren't as squeaky clean as everyone thinks, while naughty Nicky admits to having nicked a hotel bathrobe from Rome! 'Oh, and I always take the shoe polish and the gel.'

Living in each others' pockets can have its ups and downs, though. 'We've had one or two little rows with each other on this tour. It's inevitable when you're stuck with each other for weeks on end. Nothing serious but I'm not going into details,' says Kian mysteriously. Shane points out that everyone argues from time to time, 'but we're all pulling together. We're still getting to know each other and know what we do and don't like and how far we can push each other.' At any rate it's worth it for, as Mark points out, 'This is the best job you can have.'

Bryan is king of needling the others and if he knows someone's having a bad day he can really annoy them, though he says different. 'If I found out that something I was doing was really annoying the lads, I wouldn't keep doing it.'

But they do know how to have a laugh. 'At first we used to go out every weekend and have a few drinks, but now the job's taking up more and more time and it's the most important thing in the world for us,' reveals Shane. Nicky agrees. 'We're just normal lads acting the way we think we should. And it doesn't matter what people think because the fans know this is how we are and that it's natural...'

Being away from home does have its problems for the boys. Kian for one would like a girlfriend. 'It's quite lonely being on the road so much. It'd be really good to be able to pick up the phone and have a nice chat, but I don't have that.' But the boys are always there for each other when the going gets tough. 'Every couple of weeks we have a chat to make sure everyone is still grounded and that no-one's got any problems they need to sort out,' explains Nicky.

All five have completely different personalities and they complement each other most of the time. Mark is definitely the shyest band member, though he's now very relaxed with the rest of the gang. Bryan and Kian are the loudest while Kian, the best at chatting up ladies, admits he loves clothes and dressing up and never goes out without ensuring he looks 100 per cent perfect. 'I even lay my clothes out the night before to check everything goes together.'

But at the end of the day the Westlife lads have a great time together. 'The whole thing's completely fantastic! It's like a 24-hour holiday – except there's lots of work to do!' says Kian. Even when they go home to Ireland they still go out together and if there's a chance of a shopping trip the boys will be front of the queue. Last time they were in Glasgow Nicky and Kian went into town and thought nobody would recognise them in tracksuit bottoms, old tops and baseball caps, 'but we were kidding ourselves. Every shop we went into they were playing our records!'

The Westlife guys really will be mates forever and their relationship will just go on getting stronger like their music. 'The five of us have a great relationship – a strong friendship. We all love each other like brothers. I know all bands say that but we do,' says Kian. Long may that love continue!

Nicky

Name:	Nicholas Bernard James Adam Byrne
Date of birth:	9 October 1978
Place of birth:	Dublin
Lives now:	Baldoyle, Dublin, with parents
Colour of eyes:	Blue
Colour of hair:	Brown
Height:	5ft 9½ in
Hobbies:	Football and snooker
Likes:	Football (especially Man U and Leeds where he was the junior team goalkeeper), eating out, shopping and travelling home to Ireland to see his family
Dislikes:	Smoking and nasty people
Fave sports:	Soccer and snooker
Fave actors:	Bruce Willis and Brad Pitt
Fave actress:	Demi Moore
Best movies ever:	'Titanic', 'Die Hard'
Fave place to chill:	My couch in my front living room in Dublin
Fave one-liner:	How do you like your eggs in the morning?

Irish eyes were certainly smiling on the five boys from the Emerald Isle when they launched their careers as pop stars. Unlike many bands, Westlife jumped from obscurity to superstardom in the space of only a few months.

After opening a Backstreet Boys gig in Dublin, the boys began a whirlwind of promotional tours and TV appearances which culminated in November with the Smash Hits Tour and party. 'We started the campaign in October '98 before 'Swear It Again' was released and we spent so much time in people's faces that by the time the song was released everyone knew us!' reveals Mark. Shane never expected to be here in England performing. 'Doing the Boyzone tour was amazing, then we did the Smash Hits Tour and the Poll Winners' Party, which was just incredible,' he confirms.

Their hard work was rewarded as they were voted Best New Tour Act of 1998 against some stiff competition. 'A lot of bands started at the same time, so it was tricky for all of us. When Five started, there was a lull in the market, same with Boyzone,' says Shane. 'But we were competing with established acts as well as new bands like A1 and S Club 7. I think it would have been easier if we'd started in 2000.' Westlife also scooped the 'TV Hits' best band of the year. 'We haven't even released a single, but the reaction we've been getting is brilliant,' said Kian after receiving the award.

In April 1999 the band released 'Swear It Again', the long-awaited debut single, which went straight in at Number 1 in both the Irish and UK charts. Westlife had made it – and made it big time! After its release the boys continued their gruelling schedule of promo tours and TV appearances, including a memorable appearance on Ant & Dec's 'SMTV' where Mark was running down the stairs to say hello to S Club 7 but couldn't stop as he was called to go on stage. 'I ran off, tripped over a carrier bag and fell flat on my face.

westlife
TOP
OF THE
POPS

The string of Number 1 singles
that wrote Westlife's name
in the history books

I was so embarrassed – S Club were wetting themselves.'
August 1999 saw the release of single number two –
'If I Let You Go', another romantic number. That too went
speeding into the charts to land on the top spot in
both the UK and Ireland yet again. Westlife were
becoming increasingly popular with fans who
queued for hours to catch a glimpse of their
idols. 'It's getting manic in the UK,' admitted
Nicky. 'We did a TV appearance the other
day and there were loads of girls stood
outside peering through the studio
window. Four of them fainted, so the
TV people were telling us to move
away from the window.'
Just two months later
Westlife released their third
single, 'Flying Without Wings',
a song that RCA's A&R man
Simon Cowell had been keen
for the boys to record before
he'd even heard it! 'There
was this rumour about a
new song and everyone who
heard it said it was brilliant.
The chance of finding a
brilliant new song is about
one in a million, but it turned
out it was,' he explains. No
prizes for guessing at what
number it entered the chart
– yep, numero uno! Better
still the song would be
voted Record Of The Year in
December, proving the boys
weren't just pretty faces but
capable of putting across a
tune too! 'People aren't voting
on how we look,' chortled Bryan.
'"Flying Without Wings" would have
been a hit even if it had been sung
by five fat, old men instead of five fat,
young ones, heh-heh!'
In November Westlife's self-titled
debut album made its appearance and
reached a highly respectable Number 2 in the
UK charts. The album was packed with 17 fantastic
tracks – all of them potential singles material. 'We
tried to make every track on the album a single. People
will characterise them as another boy band, but Westlife are
incredible!' said Simon Cowell.
Not content with three Number 1s and a top-selling album,

westlife
TOP
OF THE
POPS

Westlife released their fourth single, the double-sided 'Seasons In The Sun'/'I Have A Dream' in time for the big Christmas showdown. It zoomed straight in at pole position on 19 December and was still there on 26 December, winning it the distinction of being the last Number 1 of the century. Even more astoundingly, it was top dog in the first week of January too, making it the first UK chart-topper of the 21st century. The boys were delighted and amazed. 'I don't think any of us expected four Number 1 singles straight off,' explained Shane. 'We were hoping for our first to go in the Top 20, so we couldn't believe it. I don't think it's anything other than hard work and luck. We did a lot of promotion, every TV programme twice, that sort of thing.'

After their fantastic singles success, the band started the New Year with a much-needed holiday in Mexico before whipping over to the US when 'Swear It Again' gave them their Stateside recording debut on 22 February. Then it was back to the UK for more promo work and the release of their next single, 'Fool Again', on 3 April which also entered the charts at Number 1 – amazing! But all this hasn't changed the boys at all. 'Everyone expected success to go straight to our heads,' says Shane. 'I think they thought we would be walking around thinking we were brilliant, but we're still the same down-to-earth lads that we've always been and always will be.'

The year 2000 is shaping up to be even bigger than 1999 for Westlife and we reckon that the best is yet to come. We may just be about to witness a boy band breaking all those records set by that other feisty five, the Spice Girls – 'cos Westlife have certainly got what it takes!

What's he like?

What the boys really think about each other – in their own words!

'Nicky tries to be the male version of Posh Spice! He likes posh clothes – he's a Gucci freak! We go to mad parties, whereas he likes going out for posh meals.'
Bryan

'Everyone thinks Shane is like Ronan, but he's very different. He shares the same charisma, but he's more like Brian Backstreet – he does a lot of lead vocals but he's not that upfront.'
Bryan

'Kian gets picked on the most because if us four are having a slagging match he never gets involved – so we can pick on him and he doesn't answer back!'
Bryan

'Mark is quite reserved. In an interview he might come across as shy, but once he gets going he's not at all. He's the strong, silent type.'
Shane

'I'd probably go to Nicky for advice before anyone else.'
Bryan

'I get on really well with everyone but I share rooms with Kian and when I go home Kian and I will go out to a club or whatever.'
Shane

'Bryan's a real softy, but he just can't help putting his foot in it!'
Shane

'I'm probably closest to Bryan because we're both from Dublin. We all get on really well, but the other three are from Sligo and you know how it is when you meet someone from the same town as you. Bryan and I room together; we relate to each other really well.'
Nicky

'Bryan and Kian are the loudest of the band. I have to tell them to be quiet a lot. But I don't get pushed around – I give just as good as I get.'
Mark

'Bryan leaves his clothes wherever he goes. There are bits of Bryan all over Europe!'
Shane

'Bryan's fine – he's just got a bit of a cheeky side. Okay, make that a big cheeky side.'
Mark

'Mark's quite reserved, but once you get to know him he's mad in the head!'
Nicky

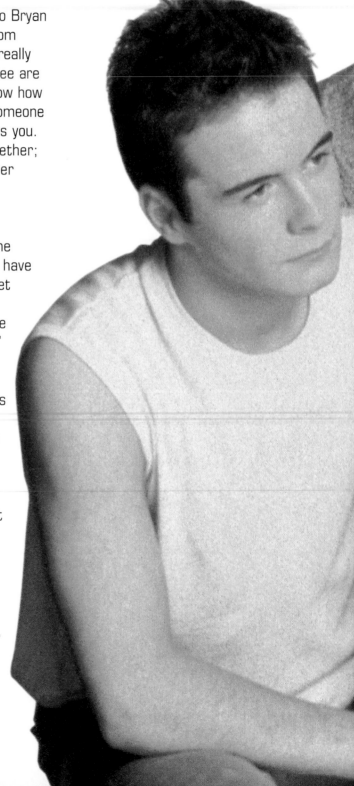

What's he like?

'Kian's the little Romeo of the band. He's a bit of a ladies' man.'
Bryan

'Shane's moody and has a short attention span, but not in a bad way. He has no bad points.'
Kian

'Even if we go home, Nicky and I always go out together. We're like family.'
Bryan

'People always like to label one in a band the wild one. Bryan's done a couple of naughty things so people call him the mad one.'
Nicky

'Nicky's the most stylish fella in the group.'
Shane

'I wouldn't like to be stuck in a lift with Nicky. He's got a bit of a phobia about them, so I don't think he'd be much fun. He'd go crazy and I'd have to look after him.'
Kian

'Nicky's a cross between Ronan and Kevin from Backstreet Boys – levelheaded, with a lot of charisma.'
Bryan

'Shane is quite laid back. He's definitely not moody, he just likes to have time to think sometimes.'
Nicky

'Kian changes his personality depending on who he's chatting up. When he's chatting up a girl he's different than when he's with us. He's smooth!'
Bryan

'If someone mistook Nicky for Ronan, it would depend on the sort of mood he was in. Sometimes he would pretend he was Ronan and other times he wouldn't.'
Mark

'Mark is the quiet, shy one of the band until you get to know him. When he first meets someone he'll sit there all quiet, but once he knows you he'll chat again.'
Shane

'Bryan is very funny. He knows how to put a smile on your face and he's a good mate. We room together and talk about things, but he's very hard to get up in the mornings!'
Nicky

'Kian is like Mark Owen and Rich from Five – the cheeky, cute one with a little bit of Stephen Gately as well.'
Bryan

Kian

Name:	Kian John Francis Egan
Date of birth:	29 April 1980
Place of birth:	Sligo, Ireland
Lives now:	On the road
Colour of eyes:	Blue
Colour of hair:	Blond
Height:	5ft 10in
Hobbies:	Snooker, pitch and putt
Likes:	Performing on stage, having a good night out and being in Westlife
Dislikes:	Sushi and rude people
Fave sport:	Basketball
Fave actor:	Brad Pitt
Fave actress:	Cameron Diaz
Best movie ever:	'Titanic'
Fave place to chill:	In front of TV
Fave place to visit:	USA
Fave one-liner:	Don't use any

The A-Z of westlife

Discovering the secret life of the Westlife boys is as easy as ABC... in our alphabetical rundown of funny, fanciful and far-fetched facts.

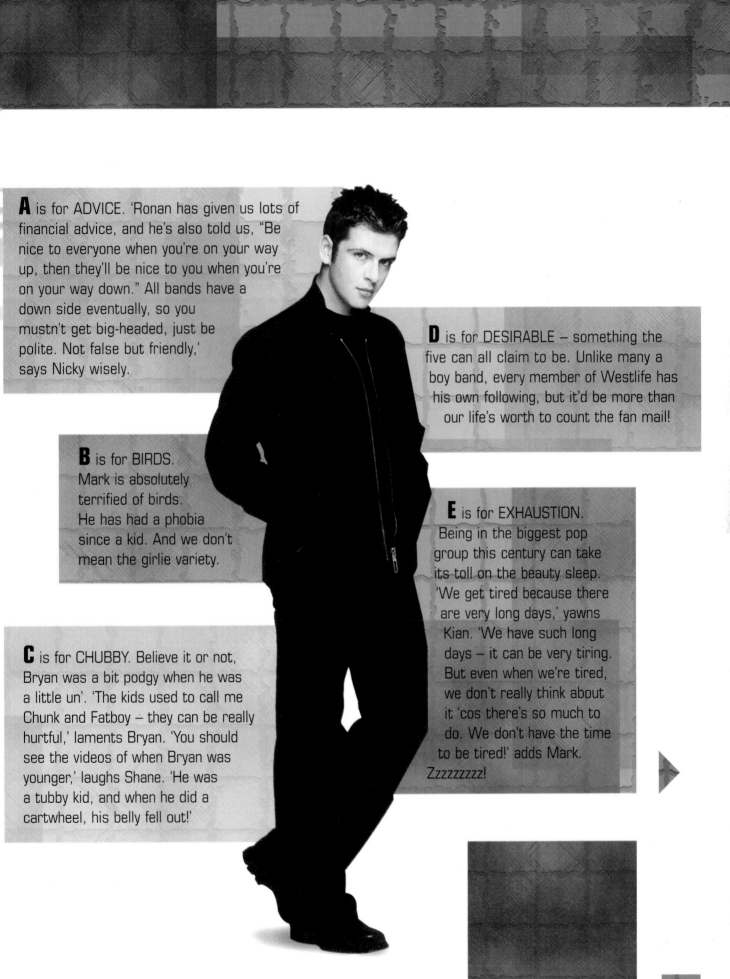

A is for ADVICE. 'Ronan has given us lots of financial advice, and he's also told us, "Be nice to everyone when you're on your way up, then they'll be nice to you when you're on your way down." All bands have a down side eventually, so you mustn't get big-headed, just be polite. Not false but friendly,' says Nicky wisely.

B is for BIRDS. Mark is absolutely terrified of birds. He has had a phobia since a kid. And we don't mean the girlie variety.

C is for CHUBBY. Believe it or not, Bryan was a bit podgy when he was a little un'. 'The kids used to call me Chunk and Fatboy – they can be really hurtful,' laments Bryan. 'You should see the videos of when Bryan was younger,' laughs Shane. 'He was a tubby kid, and when he did a cartwheel, his belly fell out!'

D is for DESIRABLE – something the five can all claim to be. Unlike many a boy band, every member of Westlife has his own following, but it'd be more than our life's worth to count the fan mail!

E is for EXHAUSTION. Being in the biggest pop group this century can take its toll on the beauty sleep. 'We get tired because there are very long days,' yawns Kian. 'We have such long days – it can be very tiring. But even when we're tired, we don't really think about it 'cos there's so much to do. We don't have the time to be tired!' adds Mark. Zzzzzzzzz!

F is for FRY-UPS which Kian can't get enough of. 'Nothing sets you up for the day like a fry-up,' says Kian. 'Rashers, sausage, beans, tomatoes, eggs, toast, tea, the whole shebang! Yum!'

H is for HÄAGEN DAZS. The boys all absolutely love ice-cream, especially the posh Haagen Dazs brand. Their favourite flavour is cookies and cream.

G is for GARDA. Nicky was going to be a policemen and has even passed all the Garda exams. He was about to join the force when he found out he was going to be in the group.

I is for IMPERSONATION. Nicky once pretended to be Ronan Keating at a gig so he could get backstage. When Ronan arrived the security guards wouldn't let him in because they thought he was the imposter. Ooops!

J is for JOKERS. Kian and Bryan are the mischievous element of Westlife and they can always bring a smile to the other 'Lifers' faces. They used to compete together for the ladies but now they team up, like Batman and Robin!

westlife

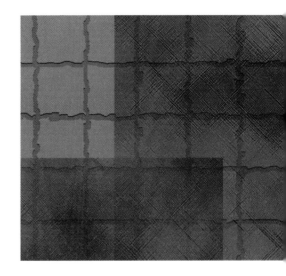

K is for KISSAGRAM. Kian used be a kissagram before the band but when the papers got hold of the story they twisted the truth and said he was a stripper. 'The guys helped me laugh at it. I mean, what else could I do? But I wasn't a stripper – I was a kissagram, and I only did it twice!'

M is for MARRIAGE. None of the boys can get married or have kids for five years according to their Westlife contract. 'The no marriage clause was more of a gentlemen's agreement. The fact is, our management know we're not going to stop going out with girls for the next five years,' explains Shane. Nicky got into trouble when his girlfriend found out about it in the Irish papers! 'But she's fine about it now. Neither of us would have thought about getting married in the next five years anyway,' he adds.

L is for LUCKY. Mark carries a lucky charm wherever he goes. 'I've got a thing like two teabags on a string – a scapular. It's like a charm – it's meant to protect you. I take it with me everywhere.'

N is for NAKED. Naughty Bryan is always getting into scrapes wherever he goes and his holiday was no exception. 'I was in Spain with my mates and they decided to strip me naked and push me out the bedroom.'

O is for OUR FATHER. Shane is a good Catholic and never goes to bed without saying his prayers and goes to church on Sundays. 'If I miss a week I feel really bad.'

R is for ROW. Being cooped up together does cause the odd bit of argy bargy on occasion. 'One week, we were killing each other because we were getting everything out of our system!' admits Kian. 'We don't ever argue properly – we just sit down and tell each other what's wrong,' says Mark.

P is for PRAYERS. Before a performance the boys have a special routine – they gather round in a circle while somebody says a prayer, then they say a quick Hail Mary and count to three in Irish before running on stage.

S is for STALKER. Kian has had someone following him around. 'It's a nightmare. She'll go to any lengths to be where I am and even follows me to the shops.' Whoever you are, let Kian pick his pizza in peace!

Q is for QUIVERING WRECK. Nicky has loads of phobias which turn him to jelly. 'I've got about 110 phobias,' quivers Nicky. 'I hate lifts. Glass ones aren't so bad but I'd crack up if I got stuck in one I couldn't see out of.'

T is for TACKLE. Bryan broke his nose playing footie when he was 12. He performed a dodgy tackle on a player who then punched him in the nose, breaking his hooter.

westlife

U is for UNDERWEAR. Nicky won't wear anything under his trousers other than genuine Calvin Klein boxers – size medium! Saucy devil!

V is for VANITY. Bryan reckons Kian is the vainest one of the group. 'I once snogged three girls in one night,' says the lad who claims he's not vain.

W is for WILD CHILD. Bryan has a reputation as the band's wild child. He once smashed up a hotel wardrobe while he was wrestling with the other lads while they were on tour. 'We got away with it, though, and I didn't do it deliberately.'

X is for X-RAY. Nicky missed the first week of school because of a car accident. 'The night before he was due to start school he got knocked down outside the house. We had to get an ambulance to take him to hospital and he had three stitches in his head,' says mum.

Y is for YUMMY. 'I'm probably the bravest when it comes to trying different food,' says Nicky. 'I love Japanese, Thai and Italian food. But the other guys are like, "Nah, just give me a burger and chips."' He does draw the line at snails, though!

Z is for ZONKED. Kian challenged Bryan for the role of party animal when he was the last member to leave the after-show party when they played in Dublin. 'All the other guys bottled out and went to bed,' he declared at two in the morning. He then went on dancing the night away until 4am when he finally zonked out!

Shane

Name:	Shane Steven Filan
Date of birth:	5 July 1979
Place of birth:	Sligo, Ireland
Lives now:	Sligo/on the road with band
Colour of eyes:	Hazel/green
Colour of hair:	Dark brown
Hobbies:	Horseriding, snooker, pitch and putt
Likes:	Shopping, girls, going out with his friends, horses and singing
Dislikes:	Insects and snakes, rude people
Fave sports:	Soccer and horseriding
Fave actor:	Tom Cruise
Fave actress:	Catherine Zeta Jones
Best movie ever:	'Titanic'
Fave place to chill:	At home
Fave place to visit:	Tenerife
Fave one-liner:	Too many to mention

Star-Crossed Lovers

Westlife may be stars themselves but what's in their stars? We take a look at their star signs and how they affect their love life.

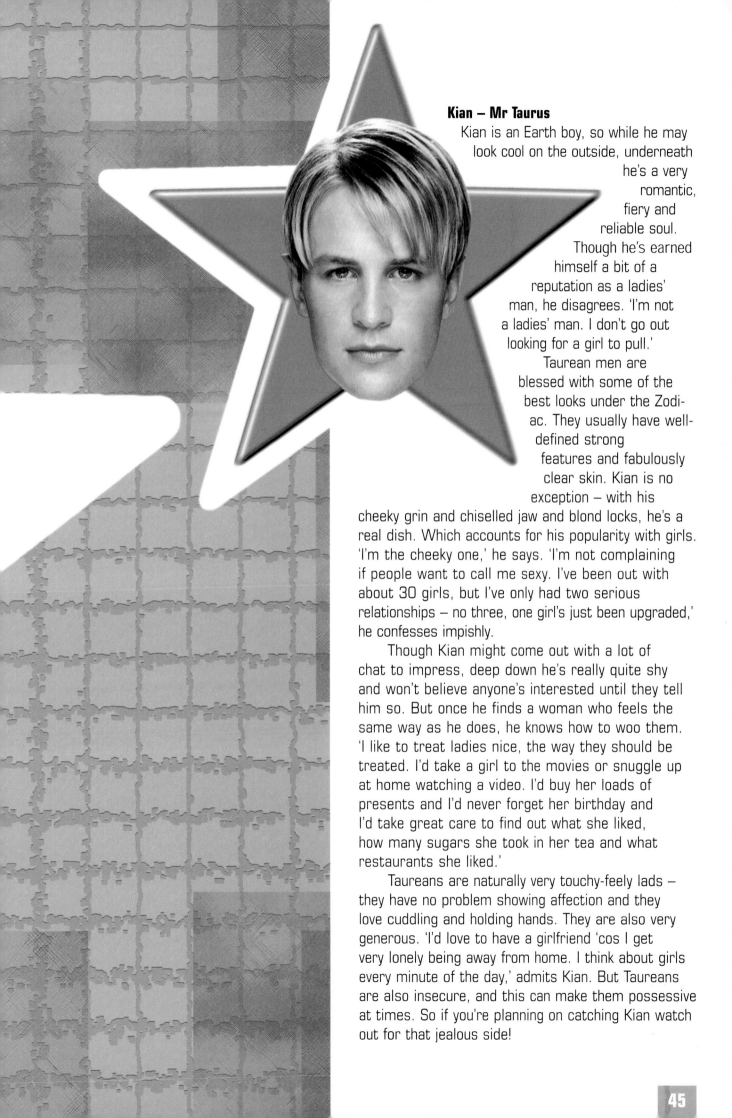

Kian – Mr Taurus

Kian is an Earth boy, so while he may look cool on the outside, underneath he's a very romantic, fiery and reliable soul. Though he's earned himself a bit of a reputation as a ladies' man, he disagrees. 'I'm not a ladies' man. I don't go out looking for a girl to pull.' Taurean men are blessed with some of the best looks under the Zodiac. They usually have well-defined strong features and fabulously clear skin. Kian is no exception – with his cheeky grin and chiselled jaw and blond locks, he's a real dish. Which accounts for his popularity with girls. 'I'm the cheeky one,' he says. 'I'm not complaining if people want to call me sexy. I've been out with about 30 girls, but I've only had two serious relationships – no three, one girl's just been upgraded,' he confesses impishly.

Though Kian might come out with a lot of chat to impress, deep down he's really quite shy and won't believe anyone's interested until they tell him so. But once he finds a woman who feels the same way as he does, he knows how to woo them. 'I like to treat ladies nice, the way they should be treated. I'd take a girl to the movies or snuggle up at home watching a video. I'd buy her loads of presents and I'd never forget her birthday and I'd take great care to find out what she liked, how many sugars she took in her tea and what restaurants she liked.'

Taureans are naturally very touchy-feely lads – they have no problem showing affection and they love cuddling and holding hands. They are also very generous. 'I'd love to have a girlfriend 'cos I get very lonely being away from home. I think about girls every minute of the day,' admits Kian. But Taureans are also insecure, and this can make them possessive at times. So if you're planning on catching Kian watch out for that jealous side!

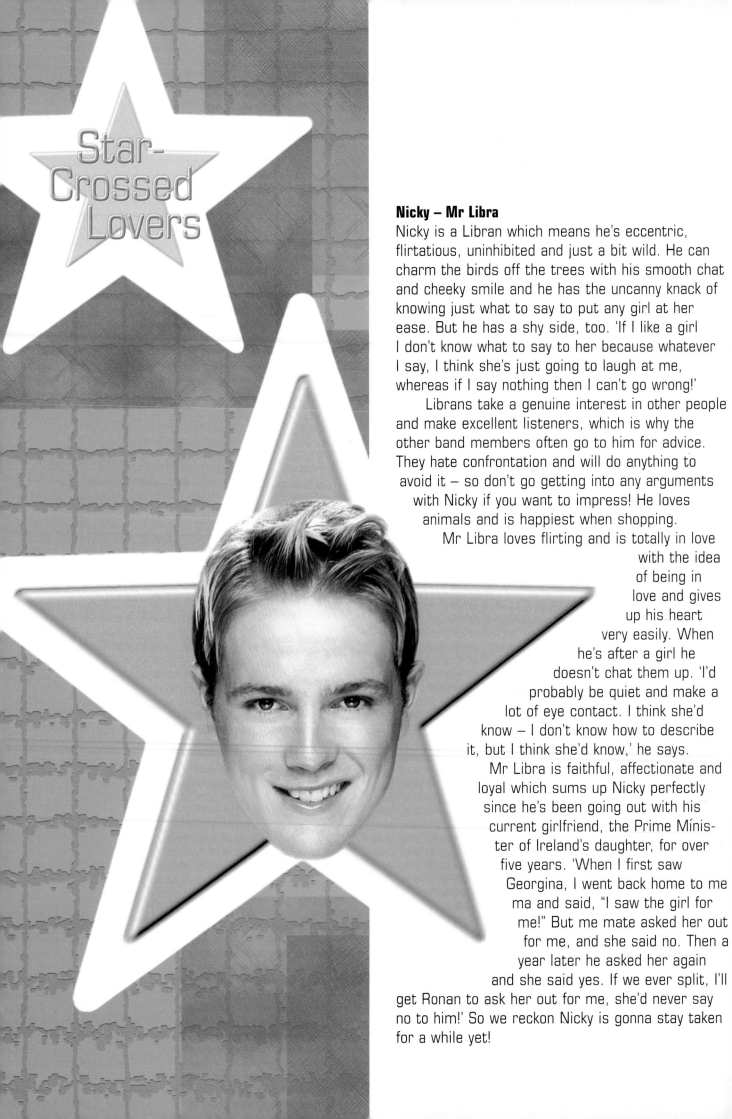

Star-Crossed Lovers

Nicky – Mr Libra

Nicky is a Libran which means he's eccentric, flirtatious, uninhibited and just a bit wild. He can charm the birds off the trees with his smooth chat and cheeky smile and he has the uncanny knack of knowing just what to say to put any girl at her ease. But he has a shy side, too. 'If I like a girl I don't know what to say to her because whatever I say, I think she's just going to laugh at me, whereas if I say nothing then I can't go wrong!'

Librans take a genuine interest in other people and make excellent listeners, which is why the other band members often go to him for advice. They hate confrontation and will do anything to avoid it – so don't go getting into any arguments with Nicky if you want to impress! He loves animals and is happiest when shopping.

Mr Libra loves flirting and is totally in love with the idea of being in love and gives up his heart very easily. When he's after a girl he doesn't chat them up. 'I'd probably be quiet and make a lot of eye contact. I think she'd know – I don't know how to describe it, but I think she'd know,' he says.

Mr Libra is faithful, affectionate and loyal which sums up Nicky perfectly since he's been going out with his current girlfriend, the Prime Minister of Ireland's daughter, for over five years. 'When I first saw Georgina, I went back home to me ma and said, "I saw the girl for me!" But me mate asked her out for me, and she said no. Then a year later he asked her again and she said yes. If we ever split, I'll get Ronan to ask her out for me, she'd never say no to him!' So we reckon Nicky is gonna stay taken for a while yet!

Mark – Mr Gemini

Like Nicky, Mark is an air sign which means he's cheeky, great fun and has his own unique brand of sex appeal. Most Gemini men have small, cute elf-like faces and Mark, with his big blue eyes and dark brown hair, is no exception.

Geminis live life to the full and will talk the hind leg off a donkey once they get to know you. His Westlife pals agree. 'Mark is the quiet shy boy of the band,' says Shane. 'Until you get to know him,' adds Kian. 'When he first meets someone, he'll sit there all quiet but once he feels relaxed he'll chat away happily,' says Shane. He hates to be turned down so he won't make a move until he's sure his feelings are reciprocated. 'Love is when you would do absolutely anything for that person. If you love someone, and they said one thing, and a thousand people said the opposite, you'd still be on their side – you'd be behind them all the way. I think the worst thing ever would be to be in love with someone and not be loved back by them...'

Mark loves flirting, but don't expect him to go rushing into a relationship quickly. Once committed Geminis stay loyal and are family-oriented. They're quite romantic, too. 'Probably the most romantic thing I've done is when I bought two tickets to the cinema and then went to eat. After I walked her home. It was really nice and cuddly, y'know?' he confesses shyly. But don't expect him to remember birthdays or anniversaries 'cos those born under the sign of the twins are notoriously forgetful.

Mark isn't in love at the moment. The last person he said 'I love you' to was his mother, so you could be in with a chance! But don't expect wedding bells from him. 'I've no plans whatsoever to get married – I'm only 18, so commitment and all that stuff is out of the window until I'm in my 30s and 40s. People are getting married when they're 65, these days. When the time is right I'll do it,' he says. Shucks!

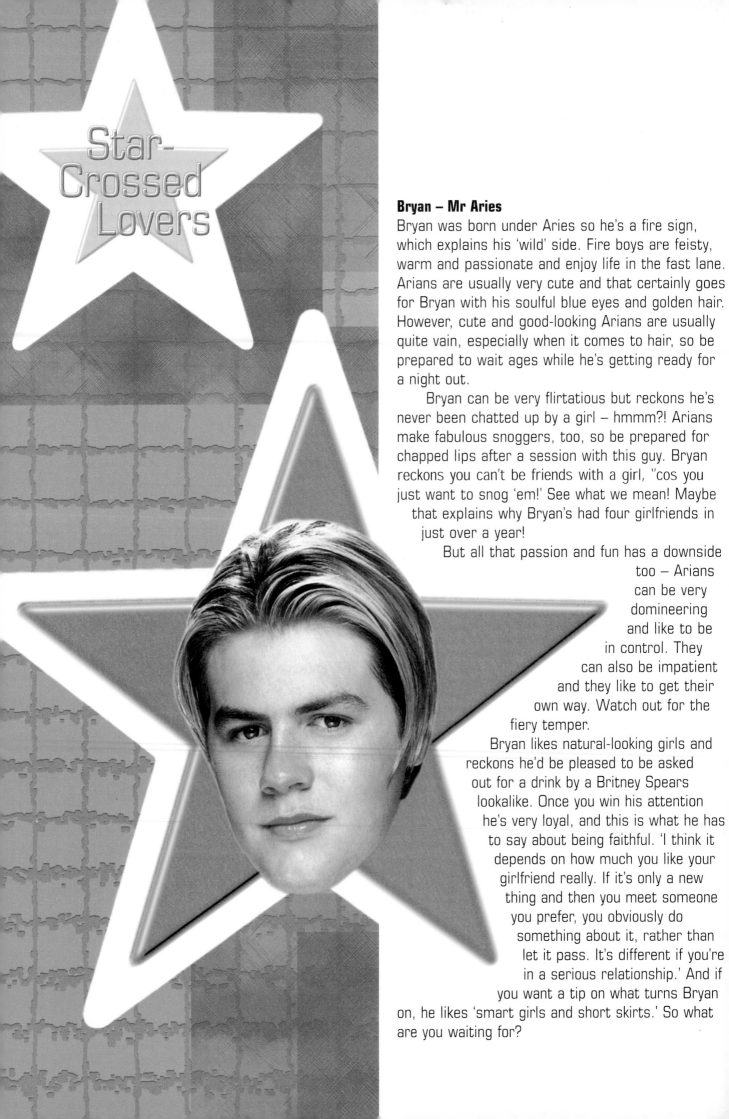

Star-Crossed Lovers

Bryan – Mr Aries

Bryan was born under Aries so he's a fire sign, which explains his 'wild' side. Fire boys are feisty, warm and passionate and enjoy life in the fast lane. Arians are usually very cute and that certainly goes for Bryan with his soulful blue eyes and golden hair. However, cute and good-looking Arians are usually quite vain, especially when it comes to hair, so be prepared to wait ages while he's getting ready for a night out.

Bryan can be very flirtatious but reckons he's never been chatted up by a girl – hmmm?! Arians make fabulous snoggers, too, so be prepared for chapped lips after a session with this guy. Bryan reckons you can't be friends with a girl, "cos you just want to snog 'em!' See what we mean! Maybe that explains why Bryan's had four girlfriends in just over a year!

But all that passion and fun has a downside too – Arians can be very domineering and like to be in control. They can also be impatient and they like to get their own way. Watch out for the fiery temper.

Bryan likes natural-looking girls and reckons he'd be pleased to be asked out for a drink by a Britney Spears lookalike. Once you win his attention he's very loyal, and this is what he has to say about being faithful. 'I think it depends on how much you like your girlfriend really. If it's only a new thing and then you meet someone you prefer, you obviously do something about it, rather than let it pass. It's different if you're in a serious relationship.' And if you want a tip on what turns Bryan on, he likes 'smart girls and short skirts.' So what are you waiting for?

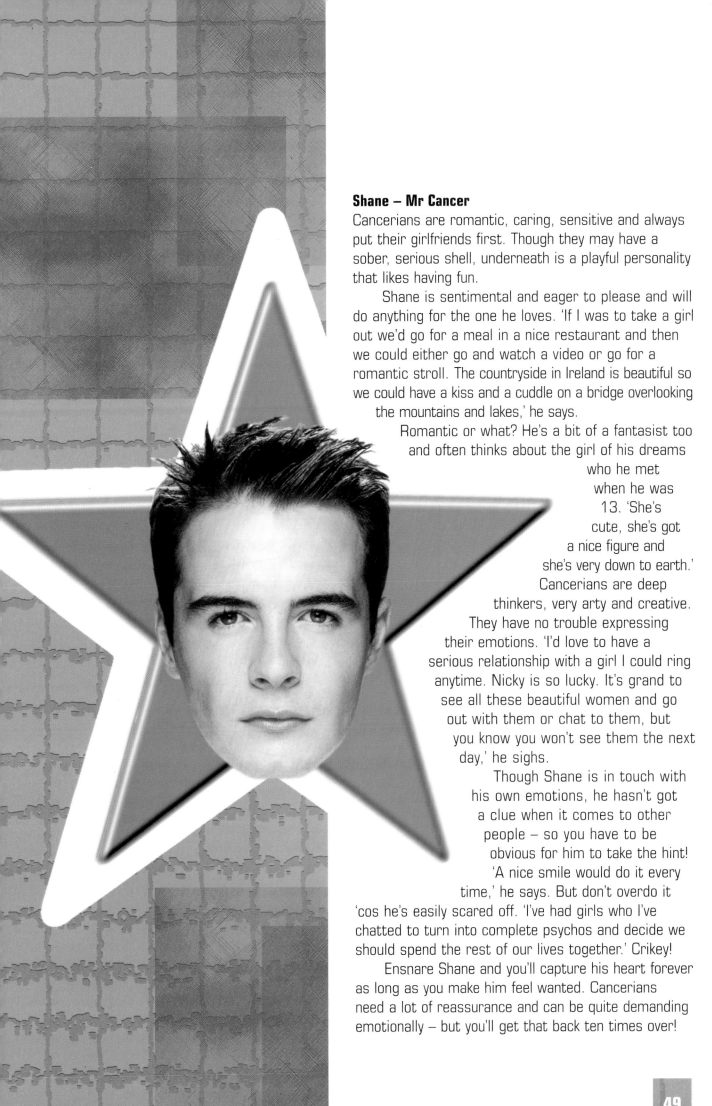

Shane – Mr Cancer

Cancerians are romantic, caring, sensitive and always put their girlfriends first. Though they may have a sober, serious shell, underneath is a playful personality that likes having fun.

Shane is sentimental and eager to please and will do anything for the one he loves. 'If I was to take a girl out we'd go for a meal in a nice restaurant and then we could either go and watch a video or go for a romantic stroll. The countryside in Ireland is beautiful so we could have a kiss and a cuddle on a bridge overlooking the mountains and lakes,' he says.

Romantic or what? He's a bit of a fantasist too and often thinks about the girl of his dreams who he met when he was 13. 'She's cute, she's got a nice figure and she's very down to earth.' Cancerians are deep thinkers, very arty and creative. They have no trouble expressing their emotions. 'I'd love to have a serious relationship with a girl I could ring anytime. Nicky is so lucky. It's grand to see all these beautiful women and go out with them or chat to them, but you know you won't see them the next day,' he sighs.

Though Shane is in touch with his own emotions, he hasn't got a clue when it comes to other people – so you have to be obvious for him to take the hint! 'A nice smile would do it every time,' he says. But don't overdo it 'cos he's easily scared off. 'I've had girls who I've chatted to turn into complete psychos and decide we should spend the rest of our lives together.' Crikey!

Ensnare Shane and you'll capture his heart forever as long as you make him feel wanted. Cancerians need a lot of reassurance and can be quite demanding emotionally – but you'll get that back ten times over!

Mark

Name:	Mark Michael Patrick Feehily
Date of birth:	28 May 1980
Place of birth:	Sligo, Ireland
Lives now:	Sligo
Height:	5ft 11in
Colour of eyes:	Blue
Colour of hair:	Dark brown
Hobbies:	Tennis, football, snooker, chilling out
Likes:	Chillin' with his mates, singing and partying
Dislikes:	Being tied down, having too much on his plate, narrow-minded people, smoking
Fave sports:	Football and tennis
Fave actor:	Eddie Murphy
Fave actress:	Lisa Kudrow (Phoebe in 'Friends')
Best movie ever:	'The Nutty Professor'
Fave place to chill:	On the couch in front of the TV
Fave place to visit:	Home (Sligo)
Fave one-liner:	Here love, here's 2 kroner – ring your mum and tell her you won't be home!

The westlife Superfan Challenge

So, you call yourself a Westlife fan? Well, let's put you to the test in our Superfan Challenge. It's simple – the more you score, the more you adore!

1. **What name did Westlife originally call themselves?**
   a. Westpoint
   b. Westway
   c. Westside

2. **Which band member is known for his wild behaviour?**
   a. Mark
   b. Bryan
   c. Shane

3. **How many Number 1 singles had Westlife scored by the Millennium?**
   a. 4
   b. 2
   c. 3

4. **What business did Nicky set up with his father in Dublin?**
   a. Carwash
   b. Hot dog stand
   c. Karaoke

5. **Which one of the band is terrified of flapping wings?**
   a. Nicky
   b. Mark
   c. Shane

6. **How long did it take A&R man Simon Cowell to decide he wanted to sign the boys?**
   a. Ten days
   b. Thirty seconds
   c. Three weeks

7. **What was the name of the song written by Shane and Mark when they were in the band IOU?**
   a. 'Together Girl Forever'
   b. 'Together We Are'
   c. 'Be Mine Forever'

8. **Which single won the 1999 'Record Of The Year' accolade?**
   a. 'Seasons In The Sun'
   b. 'Swear It Again'
   c. 'Flying Without Wings'

The westlife Superfan Challenge

9. Which one of the boys always says his prayers at night and still goes to church?
a. Mark
b. Shane
c. Kian

10. Which famous Boyzone member helps manage the group?
a. Stephen Gately
b. Ronan Keating
c. Shane Lynch

11. What is Mark's middle name?
a. Paul
b. Patrick
c. Peter

12. Which football team did Nicky once play for?
a. Liverpool
b. Leicester
c. Leeds

13. What is the name of their fifth single?
a. 'Fools Rush In'
b. 'Fool Again'
c. 'Fooling Around'

14. Mark, Shane and Kian met while acting in which play?
a. 'Grease'
b. 'Joseph and His Amazing Technicolor Dreamcoat'
c. 'Hamlet'

15. How many tracks are on the Westlife debut album?
a. 17
b. 14
c. 22

16. Who did the boys support for two days when they were starting out?
a. S Club 7
b. B*Witched
c. Backstreet Boys

17. Which Westlifer has a Black Labrador called Sloopy?
a. Kian
b. Bryan
c. Mark

18. Who is described as the Romeo of the group?
a. Kian
b. Nicky
c. Shane

19. Whose parents run a restaurant?
a. Bryan
b. Mark
c. Shane

20. Which award did Westlife win at the Smash Hits Awards?
a. Rears of the year
b. Best Tour Act of 1998
c. Worst dressed group

21. Bryan broke his nose when younger – how?
a. Playing cricket
b. Playing croquet
c. Playing footie

The westlife Superfan Challenge

22. Who can play piano up to Grade 8?
- a. Shane
- b. Kian
- c. Mark

23. What is Nicky's biggest phobia?
- a. Flying
- b. Spiders
- c. Getting stuck in a lift

24. Which Westlifer is one of seven kids?
- a. Bryan
- b. Shane
- c. Nicky

25. Nicky goes out with a famous girlfriend – who is she?
- a. The Prime Minister of Ireland's daughter
- b. Jennifer Aniston
- c. The Prime Minister of England's daughter

Scoring

Check the answers to work out your final score... Each correct answer is worth one point. Then compare your total with our ratings below.

Are You A Superfan?

Score between 1-7
Oh, dear! Are you sure you're not a 911 follower who's dialled the wrong number? Still, all is not lost. If you're serious about becoming a fan for 'Life, then you'd better read through this book again – and carefully this time!

Score between 8-17
Not bad, not bad, but don't get cocky, you're not Mastermind yet! You've got all the records and you know the boys' names but you don't know all their deepest secrets or private dreams. Start genning up on the boys and then you can really be a fan Westlife would be proud of.

Score between 18-25
Come clean! You're Ronan Keating aren't you? Well, if you aren't you should be really chuffed 'cos you probably know more about these guys than they do themselves. Well done – you really are a Superfan!

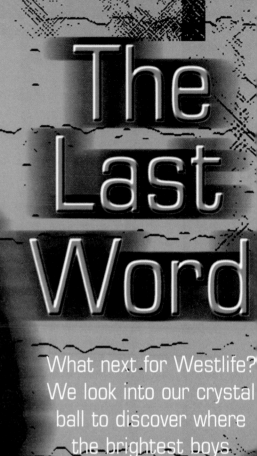

The Last Word

What next for Westlife? We look into our crystal ball to discover where the brightest boys of pop will be a year from now… ▷

The Last Word

For Westlife, 1999 was nothing if not a hectic year. They managed to release four Number 1 singles in as many months and a top-selling album, as well as receiving a number of prestigious awards. The boys have visited more countries than you've had hot dinners and mixed with the likes of Backstreet Boys, Boyzone, Baby Spice, A1 and other famous celebs. So what will the year 2000 bring, and where will they be at the end of the decade?

For a start, the year 2K is likely to see a string of further chart-topping singles – starting with their fifth in April, 'Fool Again'. There's likely to be a load of awards too. With a huge following of fans in the UK and Ireland the band is likely to look to Europe and the States for success, and you can bet they won't have to wait long to get a similar reception as they've had here.

There will be a second album at the end of the year and a tour looks likely sometime in the summer. Don't be surprised to see an awful lot of the lads on the box either, with appearances already lined up on 'The Lottery Red Alert', 'SMTV', 'Live & Kicking' and other top shows. Maybe we'll see them play at Wembley again – Nicky would certainly be thrilled. 'Playing Wembley Arena was a dream come true 'cos I always wanted to play footie at Wembley Stadium,' he says.

The boys are at last getting used to megastardom. 'We're probably the most talked-about young band,' says Shane, 'and that does sometimes scare us. But hopefully we'll just get bigger and bigger.' Nicky agrees. 'We'll just work as hard as last year, if not harder, because I don't think we can carry on with Number 1 after Number 1!'

Mark, for one, isn't put off by their increasing fame. 'It's scary, but I'm ready for whatever happens.' They all agree that they've accomplished a lot in just a few months and even if the story ended this very minute they've got so much to be proud of. 'If we retired now I don't think anyone could say anything,' says Bryan, while Mark wouldn't want the band to go

downhill. 'I know it's not likely, but you never know...' Nicky insists he'd never let that happen. 'I don't think what happened to Boyzone – where two members of the band got more attention than the rest – will happen to us. They'll always be five of us.'

But what about their private hopes and dreams? Shane has plans to build a house for his parents, while Bryan is going to buy one for his – he just hasn't got time to make one himself! For Mark, it's simply a dream come true to be in a top pop band. 'I used to look at Boyzone and say to my dad, "That's what I want to do!" But I thought there wouldn't be another big boy band from Ireland.'

All the lads agree fame and fortune won't change them. 'I won't get carried away with being a pop star,' says Shane. He believes 'you can succeed in whatever you're happy with – never worry about too much unless you have to.' For now the boys are happy to take each day as it comes. 'We don't really think about it – it's just what we are,' says Kian.

Music-wise, they will continue with the soft romantic numbers, but we'll be seeing more uptempo stuff too. 'We're already working on our dance routines,' reveals Shane with a twinkle in his eye! Kian can't see them doing any traditional Irish music, though he 'really loved that little bit in (B*witched's) "C'est La Vie" – you know, that bit with the Irish fiddle.'

Whatever they do in the years to come we reckon you're going to be hearing a whole lot more from Westlife. But one thing's for sure – these guys will never forget their roots. 'No matter how big the band gets, I know I'll always live in Ireland. At the end of the day, it's my home,' confesses Nicky. Bless 'em!